My Wall Is Red Personifies Victory
Be Inspired To Discover Who You Were Born To Be

My Wall Is Red

A Memoir of Discovery

MY WALL IS RED

A Memoir of Discovery

by Claudia DiMartino

ARPress
ILLUMINATING IDEAS,
EMPOWERING VOICES

ARPress
45 Dan Road Suite 5
Canton MA 02021
Hotline: 1(888) 821-0229
Fax: 1(508) 545-7580

Ordering Information:
Quantity sales. Special discounts are available on quantity purchases by corporations, associations, and others. For details, contact the publisher at the address above.

Printed in the United States of America.

ISBN-13:   Softcover   979-8-89389-713-5
                  eBook   979-8-89389-714-2

Library of Congress Control Number: 2024922197

Table of Contents

Dedication

This book would not have been possible without the love and prayers of family and friends. Their support gave me the courage to be vulnerable and raw as I share my life and how the Lord enabled me to tear down walls and discover my destiny through His unconditional love. My heart is to encourage others to recognize the walls that hold them back from their destiny and a deep relationship with the Lord while daring them to embrace who they are, break free from conformity, be in the moment, and live out their dreams. I thank my sister, Deborah Joyce, for her love no matter what, her honesty as she sometimes knows me better than I know myself, and for being my cheerleader as I pursue my dreams. I thank my niece, Kiera Ramirez, for being the inspiration for this book and for allowing our close relationship to give me the joy of loving her as my daughter.

I want to credit Lonnie Hughes for mentoring me in the creative process and bringing out the artist in me. I am forever grateful.

*"Set your gaze on the path before you.
With fixed purpose, looking straight ahead,
ignore life's distractions."*

(Proverbs 4:25 TPT)

Forward by Jeanie Richardson

I have known Claudia DiMartino for many years and have seen her shine as an actress in television, film and on stage. I have watched the hand of God upon her, as He has used her as a beacon of spiritual light and revelation to people in every walk of life.

Her stage show called, "It's Only Lipstick", was a moving and many times hilarious depiction of her life growing up in Brooklyn New York, in a large Italian family. But this book, My Wall Is Red, opens up new places of personal insight, intrigue, and humor, as we read of her personal discoveries, challenges, and victories.

From the first pages of this book, I was intrigued by the raw emotions, and vulnerability Claudia shares from her life stories. I was brought into a narrative that we can all relate to. It became my story. Her challenges are similar to the ones we all encounter. The life lessons and spiritual wisdom Claudia received along the way paves roads of success that we can all walk on.

From growing up in a strict Catholic home with a backdrop of shame, confusion, and insecurity, to climbing the corporate ladder of elusive success as a single woman, her resilience and determination brings inspiration, answers, and even strength to men and to women alike.

Who of us has not had our self-worth and value challenged by the actions and words of people? If your self-worth has been challenged by the assessment of people, "My Wall is Red" is for you.

Claudia begins to be brought into a living relationship with God, by supernatural experiences on her trip to Israel. You will marvel and be moved as you see how she was touched by the power of God. She thought she was going on a vacation; a recreational trip to "get away".

But as it is so often with us; she was not "getting away"; she was "coming back" to the God who made her.

This "recreation" was the beginning of her "re-creation"; she was being recreated to be used by the mighty God who called her from her mother's womb.

You will receive spiritual impartation as you read of how Claudia finds her prophetic voice as a woman of God. Her calling and confirmation from God to share His words with others is a wake-up call to us all; we are known, owned, and empowered by Him alone!

In most lives, there comes what I call, "A Crucible Moment"; This is an event or period of time in our lives that defines us; they can break us or make us. We respond by a choice to be a Victim, or a Victor. For Claudia, that happened on September 11, 2001. Claudia was close to ground zero, in New York as two jets flew into the Twin Towers. We were under attack; and so was Claudia. As she watched the unfolding of that fateful day, her paradigm was radically changed. As the towers shook and fell; so too did her earthly values of what really mattered in this life!

Claudia's journey of finding her identity and destiny in God was not to be defined by people-pleasing and performance, but rather, being free to just "be" the human "being" that God created her; to follow her heart's dreams till they became realized.

You will be strengthened in your faith as you read how Claudia comes to know and experience God's healing power. Through Claudia's faith and perseverance, she receives healing from the emotional and spiritual abuse of the past. She also sees the handprint of God in her life as she is healed physically and learns to walk again, bringing her into wholeness. Maybe you have been severely challenged and find yourself having to learn to walk again; this book is for you!

You will come to know of the God who is Your Provider. When Claudia was financially destitute, God showed himself as The Loving Heavenly Father, providing for Claudia's needs. I was moved to tears as I read of "Abba's" loving provision for her; Claudia learned she is not alone; she is not self-sufficient. She learned she can lean on the Faithfulness of Our Heavenly Father.

This is a book about discovery, discovering God and His Divine destiny for us. This book gives you permission to dream again; to believe the things that God put in your heart years ago, can actually come to pass! What is revealed in this book is the realization of God's endearing pleasure, plan, and purpose for our lives. Behind each page of this book is the echoing whisper of The God Who Made You, who alone knows the destiny you were created for. After all, He is the one who made you and put your dreams and heart-desires in you! The unfolding of Claudia's story speaks to the heart needs of every person; To be valued, irreplaceable, accepted, wanted; loved...that is you!

Jeanie Richardson

Sr. Pastor Firepoint Church

Founder, School of the Prophets

Chapter 1

The Early Years

I have come to the end of myself. I think I must have said that about 1,000 times. Then, myself would always show up. This time was different. I wrote it down in my journal. I had been sobbing for two weeks. I could not seem to stop sobbing. I would be watching a funny movie, and the floodgates would open. A cascade of tears would pour out. The most ridiculous things would trigger my emotional outbursts. Why was this time different?

I have spent a lifetime trying to figure out who I am. I always felt like I did not fit in. I exhausted so much energy trying to shoehorn myself into what everyone else wanted me to be. I did not even fit into my family. After a lifetime of trying to fit into what the world said I should be, I decided ENOUGH! It took a life-changing event to make me realize I had to get off the merry go round and go after what I wanted. Only I did not know what that was. Or so I thought.

It has taken a lifetime for me to realize I look at things differently than everyone else. It has taken a lifetime for me to realize that I am an individual; and that is a good thing. It has taken a lifetime for me to realize the advice I gave my niece twenty two years ago applied to me. I went to visit her at her apartment. She was nineteen and struggling to find her place in this world. I noticed she had painted most of the walls in her living room sage green. One wall was painted red. I asked her about her red wall. She said she wanted one wall to stand out. That struck me and we began to have a heart-to-heart chat about her life and how she looked at the world. She touched my heart. I looked at her and said, "Honey, you're not like anybody else. Your wall is red." And so many years later, I have come to realize. My Wall Is Red!

This revelation has not come easy. Since childhood, I have built another kind of wall for myself. It has been a wall of protection. I have tried to protect myself from hurt. I have tried to protect myself from disappointment. I have tried to protect myself from harsh words spoken over me. I have tried to protect myself from life. I have tried to protect myself from me. As I built up this wall of protection, it became so large that I blocked out who I am. I may have realized later in life that my wall is red, but to get there, I first I needed to tear down the walls that I built up throughout my life. Although I have come a long way, I started doubting my sanity. On the journey to discovering who I am, I took a huge step of faith. I have spent the last 22 years going after my childhood dream, and I feel no closer than I did when I started out. Oh, the pain of self-pity. How did I get here?

I grew up in a stereotypical Catholic, Italian American family in Brooklyn, NY. I am a first generation American since my dad was born in Italy. It was an extended family with three generations living in three tiny apartments under one roof. Ten completely different dysfunctional personalities all trying to survive each other and the ever-changing times of the 1960's. To be heard, you had to be loud. I was very introverted. My sister says she does not even remember me as a young kid. I was so petrified of people I would hide in closets or under beds when we had company. It always felt like everyone was fighting. My grandmother was hard of hearing. so, she was constantly screaming. Her second husband only spoke Italian. My mother and father were opposites so there was plenty of arguing. My aunt and uncle were just plain loud. They seemed to always use their outside voices inside the house. My cousins were typical boys, and my sister was the responsible one.

There was so much discipline and structure there was no room to do anything in life that was not practical and responsible. We had an intense work ethic and were shooting for the American dream. I had three Italian mamas – my mother, my aunt, and my grandmother. My mother would hit first and ask questions later. Maybe. My Aunt Dolores used the infamous wooden spoon as her weapon of warfare. My grandmother just had to be in the room. I could not get away with anything. That was tough for me because I hated structure. I wanted to burst out of the routine. My grandmother called me a "ruffiana." It was her way of calling me a free spirit. Only, with all the structure and discipline, I could not be free.

I was often punished so my response was to withdraw. I started to build my wall of protection early. It was challenging to come to terms with the fact that I was a contradiction. I was a tomboy, but I loved ballet. I was into sports and would do wheelies down the driveway on my bike. I played stickball in the street with my cousins and their friends. Yet, I could not wait to put on my tutu and go to ballet class. I hated doing chores and would trick my sister into doing them. I had a tenacious personality, but I lived in fear of authority and being punished. I think the most striking contradiction in my life was feeling like I had a split personality. I had an inner joy which was dwarfed by a daily feeling of dread. I made plans for the future but feared each day. I think about my mom. She was known for her radiant smile which lit up a room. But that smile hid so much pain. Her father rejected her because she was not a boy, and she grew up in a home filled with fighting and rage. For me, that translated to her telling me she was proud of me, but the scowl on her face spoke volumes which resonated as disapproval.

The more I withdrew, the more introverted I became. I created my own little world. I had a vivid imagination. TV and movies fed into my imagination and my ability to recreate characters from those shows. I would even make up my own stories and act them out. My family called me the little actress. My dad fed into my creative bent. Even though he had a temper and we dubbed him Mt. Vesuvius, he always made time for us. He started the Tall Tale Society. I was the president. On Saturday mornings, my cousins, my sister, and I would all crawl into bed with him and listen intently as he would make up stories and adventures on the spot. On Saturday afternoons, he would take us to the Mayfair theater where we would settle in and enjoy the double features. I loved it!

School cramped my style. Being Italian and Catholic, parochial school was the only option. The nuns were so strict. We would be physically punished if we did something wrong. I remember the time when I was in the seventh grade. The boy behind me stuck the point of a compass in my rear end. It hurt! Being the tomboy that I was, I got up and belted him. My teacher, who was a priest on sabbatical from the seminary, called me to the front of the room. He did not ask any questions. He did not want to know what triggered my aggressive behavior. Instead, he took a geography book and hit me across the face with it. I went flying into a desk. I recovered from the pain and the shock; but I did not tell my parents what happened. I learned early on in my school days that if I told my parents I was punished in school, I would get punished again at home. The teachers were always right. My wall grew with the fear of being punished.

The emotional abuse was worse. I withdrew completely. In the fourth grade, I was put in the dumb row if I got an answer wrong. I had a curious mind; but I learned early to keep my mouth shut. This had a major impact on me as I grew up. I believed I was stupid. I was afraid of making a mistake. I was afraid of authority figures. I was afraid of being punished. This was amplified when I was in the sixth grade. When it was report card day, a priest would visit each class and hand out the report cards individually to each student. I remember how nervous I was and for good reason. This day, the senior pastor of our parish came into our classroom. I could hear the collective gulp from my classmates. He was just plain cruel. My teacher rightly positioned a chair for him facing the class. One by one he called each student up front to receive their report card. Each one had to stand their quietly while the pastor read out each grade and sternly commented on grades that were not A's or B's. I was petrified. I struggled terribly in science and math. When my name was called, I slowly got up from my desk and walked apprehensively to the front of the room. I remember being humiliated as he chastened me for being lazy and not doing my best. I fought the tears that quickly filled my eyes. After this humiliation, I had to go home and show my report card to my parents. They had to sign it to prove I showed it to them.

Something wonderful happened. My parents knew I tried. My dad stepped up to the plate and hit a home run. He said he was going to teach himself math and science so he could help me with my subjects. Even though he was Mt. Vesuvius, he did not yell at me. He did not punish me. He was loving, understanding, and wanted to help me.

Unfortunately, even though my father gave so much to help me with homework, that did not translate to taking tests. I was petrified of taking tests. I was now in the eight grade, and it was time to take the standardized tests and apply to parochial high schools. My sister passed. My cousin Wayne passed. I did not pass. I felt like such a failure which was amplified because I now needed to attend public high school.

Everyone else was accepted into Catholic high schools, except me. I now added being a failure to my wall.

It was 1968, and the country was in turmoil. It was the decade where President John F. Kennedy and the year that Robert Kennedy and Dr. Martin Luther King were assassinated. It was the explosion of the Civil Rights Movement and busing was implemented in the school system. There were protests and riots against the Vietnam War. It was the hippie generation and drugs were rampant as was "free love." I often say I grew up in the backyard. I was not prepared for this "public" school experience. I wore buttondowned blouses, pleated skirts and I even put pennies in my penny loafers. I was a square peg in a round hole. I was the "good" Catholic girl. I did not do drugs. I did not drink. I did not skip school. I did not protest the war or go on moratoriums from school. And, most definitely, I did not date. I was miserable.

This just added to my nervous nature. I was a mess physically and emotionally. At the age of ten, I was tested for an ulcer. I could not eat. Minutes after eating I would run to the bathroom sick to my stomach. At first my parents thought I was just trying to get out of doing the dishes. They would make that deep sigh and laugh as if to say here she goes again. Then they realized it was happening too much to laugh at it or ignore it. This was difficult on a deeper level. My mother was an amazing cook. She showed her love through her food. She relished her family getting together and enjoying her delectable delights. Food was also used as a reward. I grew up believing that food was both a blessing and a curse. In my formative years, I developed a warped sense of food. It tasted so good, but I feared getting sick every time I ate. Add another layer to my wall. It was not until I was twenty-one that I discovered I was dealing with IBS (Irritable Bowel Syndrome). It explained so much. Ten was a rough age for another reason. Not only did I deal with serious stomach issues; I also became a "young lady." I went from being flat chested to curvaceous overnight. Since this was the era of Twiggy, I hated my body because I was not skinny. Every day it hit me in the face. My sister was tall and thin. I was short and full figured. I had such a negative body image. Adding to the misery, I dealt with intense female pain every month. I hated being a girl. I just wanted to hide. Add poor self-image to my wall.

When I was sixteen, our family doctor strongly recommended that my parents take me to see a psychiatrist. They did so reluctantly. Seeing a psychiatrist was a new concept. This was supposed to help me come out of my shell, but I felt it brought shame instead. I could hear my grandmother. "How could someone in our family need a psychiatrist?" She was a bull in a chine shop and plowed over anyone who disagreed with her or got in her way. Feelings did not matter.

I felt ashamed. I withdrew even more. The doctor could not figure me out because I just sat there. I would not talk. He brought in my parents and my sister to get a better understanding of me as a person. After a year, my parents put an end to it. He told them that they needed to get me out of that house. It was an unhealthy environment for me to be in. We were a close family. Too close. That advice went over like a lead balloon.

He did not even help me get over the feeling that I was stupid. Since the days when I was put in the dumb row, I believed I was not smart enough to take the academic program in high school. I took the commercial program instead. It was all the business stuff – bookkeeping, typing, stenography. I was able to type 120 words a minute: and I never missed a word when taking dictation. Even though I had a 95% average, I still felt like a second-class citizen. It was the commercial program not the academic program. However, I did put my skills to good use, and I worked part-time as a typist at a law firm in Manhattan. As a junior in high school, I had an early schedule. I usually got out at around 12:00; and I would take the train into the city, go to work, come home and then do my homework. I was being responsible; and I would turn my paycheck over to my parents. They would give me a portion of it as an allowance. Between school, work, and chores, I did not have too much time for fun. Instead, I lost myself in tv and movies. They were my escape. In my junior year, I discovered there was a drama class I could take as an elective class. At first, I wondered if I would get credit for the class because it seemed like it would be fun. It was. I loved it; and it brought out the acting bug in me. The acting bug I so used as an escape as a young child and later suppressed. I was too shy to audition for any of the school plays. I comforted myself thinking they were always musicals, and I knew I did not sing. It never occurred to me that there were non-singing roles. I attended the school plays and daydreamed about being on that stage. My drama teacher even encouraged me to audition; but it was safer to daydream.

The arts were important to my family. My father saw to that. We would attend plays on Broadway, go to the opera and museums. We would get all dressed up and take the car into the city, not the subway. The arts were special. And I wanted to be a part of it. So, when I was eighteen and trying to decide what would be my major in college, I decided to take the plunge. I told my parents I wanted to major in the fine arts. Dead silence. When my mother came out of shock, she said, "absolutely not." .My dad wanted to know where this was coming from. I never told them I was taking drama in school. He realized I wanted to major in acting, and the fireworks began. My mother, always the practical one, screamed, "that's insane! Acting does not put food on the table!" My dad agreed, and he said, "acting is a good hobby; but focus on a real career."

I was so disappointed; and I was so lost. I did not know what to do. I tried going to a community college for a semester, but that did not work out. I then decided to put my business skills to use; and I went to work as a secretary at Helena Rubinstein in New York City. I thought working in the cosmetics industry would be so glamorous. I worked for a career administrator who was with the company about 40 years. I did well and was moved to a department working with cosmeticians and makeup artists. Then, I got my first taste of a corporate takeover. We were sold to ColgatePalmolive; and it was not a match made in heaven. We went from our glamorous headquarters on Fifth Avenue to the more sterile environment of our new parent company. My department was tucked away in a tiny, rundown section of the building. I had to sit close to our Executive Vice President's assistant who reeked of rose scented perfume. I had a constant headache. Things just changed; and I felt I needed a change as well.

I decided to quit; and I started working at an advertising agency on Madison Avenue. I really enjoyed my job. Working in advertising, I was exposed to marketing and developing marketing plans into creative advertising campaigns. Although, I was doing well, I felt something was off. I would look around at the other administrative assistants. I felt I did not fit in. Even though I grew up in a combination blue collar/white collar home, I felt I was not the stereotypical administrative assistant. It is what I call, the doity doid street and doid avenue types. Translating the blue collar New Yorkese, that is Thirty-third Street and Third Avenue. After a year, I felt I could do more. I decided I wanted to go back to college and major in marketing, only I wanted to be the client. Upon resigning, I was offered the opportunity to work part-time at the agency while I attended school. I was pleasantly surprised; and I accepted. It felt good to be appreciated, and I figured the money would come in handy. So, I worked part-time at the agency while I attended Bernard Baruch College full-time. I graduated in February 1980 with my Bachelor of Business Administration. I felt such a sense of accomplishment, and I was ready to take on the world. Not so fast. It was the recession of 1980 and jobs were hard to come by. I could only seem to get interviews for administrative assistant jobs. I resisted. I was an administrative assistant. I went back to college to get a better job. After six months of unemployment, I interviewed at Revlon. During the get to know you part of the interview, the HR Manager asked me to take a typing and steno test. This time I thought I was interviewing for a job in marketing. I took a deep breath and said, "Excuse me?" In a sugary sweet voice, she said, "Everyone at your level must start in an administrative assistant position." Anger was rising. "My level, I just graduated with my Bachelor of Business Administration." Again, sugary sweet, "Unless you have your master's degree, you must start at the administrative assistant level."

Through gritted teeth, I took the tests; but I was so angry. All that hard work for what!?! To go backwards! I took all my frustration out on that keyboard. At that time, we used the IBM selectric typewriter. It sounded like I was shooting off a machine gun. RRRRRRRR… After taking the tests, I was, once again seated in the HR Manager's office. She was a bit befuddled. She asked me to take the typing test again. There had to be something wrong with their timer. I said, "Your timer?" "Yes, it's just not possible for anyone to type 140 words a minute with only two errors." I must confess I was a bit cocky with the news. I agreed to take the test again knowing the results would be about the same. They were exactly the same!

After that, I was set up on two interviews that day. The first interview was with a pot-bellied, balding sweaty man who had no concept of how to conduct an interview. Saying he was rude and gruff is an understatement. He looked at my resume and glared at me. He astutely said, "I guess you're looking for a position that would lead to a promotion." I was so repulsed, I had all to do to keep it together. I said, "that would be my goal." Then the unthinkable happened. He started laughing at me. I mean, LAUGHING AT ME! I was disgusted and confused at the same time. Then he laid the bomb on me. Through his guffaws, he said, "you could be at Revlon for years before being considered for a promotion." I wanted to run out screaming! Instead, I thanked him and left.

I could not believe it. I worked so hard only to be laughed at by some cog stuck in the corporate wheel. Deep inside I was screaming, "How dare he laugh at me!" Yet, it felt so familiar. I needed to take a deep breath and pull myself together. I had another interview in a few minutes. I felt dejected and just wanted to go home. Instead, I went back to the reception area and waited to be summoned for my next interview. I was not expecting much. Suddenly, I heard my name called. I looked up and there was a young woman who looked familiar to me. She smiled and said in her very thick New York accent, "Mr. O'Sullivan will see you now." I smiled and got up. I could not resist saying that she looked familiar. She said, "Yeah, you too." Then it hit me. I asked her if she had attended Baruch College. She said, "Yeah, I did." Then, she announced that she was being promoted and I was interviewing for her job. All I heard was being promoted. I asked, "How long have you been here?" She said, a year and that Mr. O'Sullivan keeps his promises about promotin' good people."

I figured this must have been a sign. I felt uplifted, and the interview with Mr. O'Sullivan went well. I felt this was the opportunity I was looking for. Only it was not. Instead of working for one person, I worked for six executives. Plus, I was often asked to cover for the assistants to the Executive Vice Presidents of both Marketing and Finance. This came with a very uncomfortable experience. One Christmas, the Executive Vice President of Finance gave me a gold initial pendant and chain as a thank you for helping him out on many occasions throughout the year. I thanked him. I went back to my desk and decided to put the pendant on as a sign that I liked it. Later in the day, he called me over. He said, "I see you're wearing the pendant." I said, "Yes, thank you again." He said, "Let me see." As I got closer to him, he reached out and pulled my blouse open. I was mortified and threw my arms across my chest. These were days before sexual harassment education and corporate behavior rules. I will never forget how he just glared at me and gave me this evil grin. He turned and went back into his office. I could not help thinking, "What did I do to deserve that?" Instead of recognizing that what he did was wrong, I immediately fell into me doing something wrong. I did not. I dressed modestly and conducted myself as lady. But the damage was done. I added another layer of being afraid of men to my wall.

I also had to deal with the very sexy, blonde secretary of the Senior Vice President of Marketing Administration. She sat right next to me. Let's just say her workload was light compared to mine. I was often asked to "pitch in." I was the one with my nose to the grindstone. I worked hard with the goal of always moving up the corporate ladder. Yet, I could not help feeling abused and taken advantage of. I could not understand why this type of thing kept happening to me. I would watch others who did not work as hard get rewarded. Did I feel I would be punished if I refused to take on other people's workload? Instead of addressing the issue with my boss, I stuffed my feelings. This is another example of how, since childhood, I did not speak up. I did not realize that as I stayed quiet, I was allowing anger to build up inside of me. My wall loomed large. I needed to do something. That something was to work even harder to get ahead.

After a year, I realized I needed to make a change. I needed to be creative and that certainly was not it. I needed to get into marketing. I had this grand illusion that marketing was my calling. I decided to take advantage of the company's tuition reimbursement program. I applied to universities to pursue my Master of Business Administration. I was accepted into Pace University's Lublin School of Business. I now gave new meaning to keeping my nose to the grindstone. I was working 65-70 hours a week while going to school three nights per week. On the bright side, my hard work paid off. I was promoted to a marketing administrator position. My boss expected nothing less than long hours to get the job done. We did have an agreement that I could leave at 5:00 on the nights I had school. I oftentimes, arrived at work early to make sure all my work was done, especially those last-minute projects.

On the day I was to take my last final exam to get my MBA, my boss came into my office and demanded I get a special project done that night for her meeting the following morning. I reminded her that I had my final that night and we agreed that I could leave by 5:00. She did not budge. I did the unthinkable. I could only focus on taking my last final for my last class. I asked her, "What time is your meeting?" She told me 10:00. I got up from my desk and told her I would come in early the next morning to do it for her, as I raced out of the office to get to class. I thought I would get fired, but I needed to stay focused. In the words of Scarlett O'Hara, "I'll think about it tomorrow."

I arrived at my class, sat down, and took my final. I put my pen down and handed in my exam. It took everything I had to keep my emotions in check. Then, there was the long ride home on the express bus. I put my key in my apartment door and fell on the sofa. The floodgates of emotion began pouring out. I started laughing and crying at the same time. "I did it. I did it!" It was midnight; and I felt I wanted to celebrate my achievement. I was given a mini bottle of champagne when I bought my sofa. My dad was an architect, and I was allowed access to the designer showrooms on Madison Avenue. It was their way of saying thank you. I opened the bottle, poured myself a glass, stood up and said, "Salute!" Since I do not drink, I think that's the best night's sleep I ever got. I just crashed. Thankfully, I was able to get up the next morning to get to work early to do that report. But that was not my only celebration. I wanted to celebrate in style.

Chapter 2
Spiritual Awakening

Growing up Catholic and surviving the discipline of the nuns and priests, I did not understand the love of God. I really did not understand the sacrifice Jesus made on my behalf. I knew about Jesus; but I did not know Jesus. I would attend church every week and go to confession. That is what Catholics do. I obeyed the rules. But I think even as a child, I knew there was something more. I remember sitting in church when I was about six years old. The church had the stainglassed windows; and there were the statues of saints and the sacred heart rightly positioned around the church. I remember sitting in one of the pews; and I would watch the little Italian ladies dressed in black holding their rosary beads praying and touching the statues. There was nothing joyful in their daily ritual. They seemed to be so pained and sad. As I watched this weekly ritual, I could not stop thinking, "Why are they praying to statues. They're not real." I did not dare tell anyone I had that thought. My own grandmother had a grotto to Saint Anthony in our small backyard. It just felt that something was not right.

Fast forward to 1984. It was time to celebrate getting my MBA. There were two celebrations. The first was with my family. While attending graduate school, I moved out of my parent's home, and I purchased a co-op in Sheepshead Bay, Brooklyn thanks to my dad's connections. His golfing buddies were on the board. I loved the apartment I chose, and I was able to put down twenty percent. My parents carried my "mortgage." I faithfully paid them each month without fail. To my surprise, at the family celebration, my parents handed me a bank book. I stared at it. From the day I turned sixteen and turned over my paychecks to my parents, they deposited those paychecks in that bank account. It was supposed to be part of my wedding gift from them. Since I never married, my sister insisted they give me the gift when I got my MBA. I was overwhelmed. The money in the bank book equaled what I owed my parents for my "mortgage." I owned my apartment outright.

Next was my own personal celebration. I loved to travel. I was usually spontaneous, and very rarely planned trips ahead of time. This was different. For three years, it was nothing but work and school. I had absolutely no life. I was exhausted and exhilarated at the same time. I wanted to celebrate in style. I decided to take the trip of a lifetime. I loved taking cruises. I felt safer since I often traveled alone. I tend to make decisions quickly; and I could not seem to get any friends to commit to traveling with me. If I waited for them, I never would have gone anywhere or experienced the wonderful trips and adventures around the world. This time, I planned a two-week vacation. I decided to fly to Greece for a week then cruise the Mediterranean. It would be expensive, so, I decided to take my last tuition reimbursement check and splurge. I was so excited I just had to tell my parents what I was planning. I did not get the response I hoped for.

My mom was the practical one and the penny-pincher. She could not understand doing anything that seemed irresponsible and frivolous. When I bubbled over and blurted out my exciting news, she said, "That's so expensive. How are you going to pay for it?" I revealed my grand plan of using my last tuition reimbursement check. Instead of getting that is a good idea, I got "you need furniture. Why can't you be practical for once." I am not proud of myself. I erupted. "Practical. I've been practical my whole life." Those words cut deep, and in a split second my joy evaporated. I was so angry. My dad had to intervene. My dad got it. In the early years, he worked full time and studied architecture while he attended Cooper Union at night. He was under so much stress as my mother was pregnant with my sister at the time. He had first-hand experience and understood what I had been through for three years. In his own simple, direct way, he looked at me and said, "Enjoy." I cried.

I prepared for weeks for my trip. I took care of every detail, but the detail about spending so much money kept gnawing at me. Being responsible, I laid out my budget and I kept to it. The big day arrived, and I finally winged my way to Athens, Greece. I hoped I could relax and enjoy myself; but I even had to work hard on vacation. I crammed so much into two weeks. I visited all the major tourist sites in Athens – The Parthenon, The Acropolis, Cape Sounion, Delphi, and Mycenae to name a few. It was a full schedule, but I allowed myself to be transported into an ancient world. I was like a sponge taking it all in.

While in Athens, I came face to face with my need to be financially responsible while trying to decide if I should purchase what I thought was an extraordinary piece of jewelry. My love of fine jewelry came from my grandmother. Whenever my grandmother traveled to Italy, she always came home with another piece of fine jewelry, whether it be 18K gold or diamonds. She had some eye-popping pieces. Even though my tuition reimbursement check was covering the cost of the trip, I would need to dig deep to buy a diamond and sapphire ring. I could not take my eyes off it. I tried it on. I took it off. I tried it on. I took it off. I left the store. I lingered. I went through the cost of the ring and my budget for the trip. I took out my traveler's checks and calculated the amount and how much trip I had left. Then the thought hit me that I no longer had to pay a mortgage payment to my parents each month. Their graduation gift to me rendered me free and clear of that debt. I bit my lip and a little smile appeared. I took a deep breath and decided to exercise my freedom as an adult. I went back into the jewelry store and said, "I'll take it." Instead of my traveler's checks, I used my lone credit card. This truly was a guilty pleasure. Some of the guilt subsided when I received my credit card statement the following month. The exchange rate was adjusted in my favor, and I saved a hundred dollars off the ticket price. I enjoyed that ring for many years. It was also a beautiful reminder of my trip of a lifetime.

It was a glorious week in Greece. With ring in hand, it was now time to board the ship in Piraeus. I cruised to the islands of Rhodes, Ephesus, and Patmos. At the time, I did not realize how biblically significant these places were. In Rhodes, I had a nice surprise. I met a man who was single and handsome. I was a bit awkward because I did not date much, if at all, so I was not quite sure how to act. Thankfully, our adventures during the trip offered up topics for some bubbly conversation. We seemed to hit off. As we were chatted, I discovered he was a professor of Western Civilization. Is this for real? It was like having my own personal tour guide, especially heading into Egypt and then Israel. On the island of Rhodes is the Rhodes Citadel: The Fortress of The Knights of St. John. We decided to meet up early the next morning to walk to the fortress to climb the 999 steps to watch the sunrise. Youth is definitely a good thing. We gingerly started to climb the steps and dragged a bit by the time we got to the top of the stairs. As we approached the top, we jokingly started to count the steps aloud. 995. 996. 997. 998 and 999. We made it! As we walked onto the top of the fortress, we stopped in our tracks. The view was breathtaking. The sun was coming up and the sky was filled with magnificent colors that reflected off the pure blue Mediterranean Sea. I felt like I was in a movie. A real chick flick. I was daydreaming about how things would progress. He takes my hand. We look up at the sunrise. We walk back down the steps, stop for a lovely breakfast. Not! After about an hour, He said, "Well, we better be getting back to the ship." I felt a pang of disappointment. Those innocuous words were a blow to my self-esteem and my confidence as a woman. In a split second, my mind started racing. Would I ever experience a romantic interlude? Why not me? What is wrong with me? It was as if those stairs were a symbol of my romantic life. I went up the stairs with hope and came down the stairs with disappointment. I always wanted to marry and have children. In that moment, I started to doubt if I would ever have a meaningful relationship. Here I am in a very romantic setting and nothing. I did a good job of hiding what I was thinking. I smiled and nodded in agreement that we should return to the ship. But in that moment, I added another layer of not being attractive to men to my wall. We started our descent down the steps and headed back to the ship. At least I will always have the steps and the sunrise.

The next morning, we docked in Port Said, Egypt. It was a three hour bus trip to Cairo. Driving through the desert, I was transported into ancient Egypt. As I looked out the window, I could see Bedouins on camels traveling through the desert. When we arrived in Cairo, I was stunned by the abject poverty. We were warned not to eat or drink anything until we arrived at the designated hotel for lunch. I remember driving through the market and seeing an old man dressed in black sweeping the curb outside of a food store. Dust was flying everywhere and landing on the hanging poultry and food on open display. That really opened my eyes as to why I should not eat or drink anything.

One of the first stops was the Cairo Museum. I was overwhelmed by the grandeur of the treasures of Tutankhamun. I remember laughing to myself as I stood in the middle of the exhibit. During that time, the Tutankhamun exhibit was traveling the world. I wanted to see it when it arrived in New York City. The crowds were massive and, at that time, the expense for me, was prohibitive. Now, here I am in the Cairo Museum with only my tour group looking at the treasures that crowds of people jammed into museums around the world to see.

The next stop were the pyramids at Giza and the Sphynx. I decided to travel to these historic landmarks by camel. This was not a short camel ride; and I learned that camels are mean. My tour guide advised us not to tip the camel driver until we got to the destination and got down from the camels. When I chose my camel, I jumped back as it turned its long neck to me and growled. I now doubted my decision. I took deep breath and got on the camel. This was challenging as I have short legs and I had trouble hoisting myself into the saddle. Once on the camel, my feet did not reach the stirrups and I was told to just hold on. I did. For dear life. The camel started to get up and I was thrown back and forth as it raised its hind legs and then its front legs. I thought I was going to be seasick. My camel had a bit of kick in its step and trotted along. I screamed as I realized the camel was going to jump over a small wall. The camel driver seemed to be in control; and we made it over the wall.

I arrived at the pyramids; and I was in awe. I could not take enough pictures. I avoided going into one of the pyramids because I can experience feeling claustrophobic. Instead, I stayed outside and took in the majesty of where I was. Suddenly, a sandstorm kicked up and sand was flying everywhere. I learned first-hand that sand hurts when it pelts you in the face. I was covered from head to toe with sand. I stood there in disbelief. I then started laughing when I realized where I was and that it was worth it. Growing up in New York City, tourists would flock to the city every year to marvel at the skyscrapers and all that the city had to offer. But here I am, a New York City kid, standing in front of the pyramids at Giza. I felt dwarfed by their size and history.

I got back on my camel. The next stop was the Sphinx. Awesome! Again, I could not take enough pictures. I was not satisfied with any picture. I had to get the perfect picture. I decided to go under a rope. I was so caught up in the moment I did not realize that rope was meant to keep people out. Suddenly, whistles blew, and my tour guide grabbed me and pulled me back to the other side of the rope. She kept the guards at bay and hurried me along. She said, "Get on the bus. You could be arrested." "ARRESTED! Visions of being dragged off to an Egyptian prison started floating in my brain. Panic started to set in. Handcuffs! Solitary confinement! Arabic! I hustled to get back to the bus as fast as I could. I shouted to my tour guide, "I think I am going to faint." She shouted back, "Do it on the bus!"

Once on the bus, I composed myself. The thought of being arrested freaked me out. I have always walked the straight and narrow road. The thought of doing something wrong that would land me in a foreign prison was nowhere on my radar. It is not even on my radar at home where we speak English. I needed to make a mental note to pay attention and not get so caught up in the moment. On second thought that is ridiculous. Living in the moment is what makes things special. It makes for great memories. How would I relive that memory? Almost getting arrested in a foreign country is great material for a story. Should I tell it as it happened or embellish it a little? I do not need to add anything. Even though that was exciting for all the wrong reasons, I must admit, it was worth it and worth repeating it as it happened! It enriched the phenomenal experience of walking through antiquity.

We started to make our way to the next stop which was a gift shop where we stopped enroute to Giza. At the shop, I was involved in what I thought was a rather funny experience. As evidenced with my diamond and sapphire ring purchase, I like to buy something substantial as a lasting memento of my trip. I decided to purchase a gold cartouche pendant with my name engraved in hieroglyphics. Thankfully, it was not that expensive. I was specific with my order. I wanted the pendant in brushed gold and my name in high polished gold so that the symbols would stand out. When we arrived at the jewelers to pick up our orders, I did what I always do. I examined the merchandise before I paid for it. It was not prepared to my specifications.

The entire pendant was high polished gold. I tried to explain the error to the shop owner. He yelled at me and got emotional. My tour guide came over to see what all the hub bub was about. I explained it to her. I showed her my receipt that clearly laid out what I wanted. She then took over and started to converse with the shop owner. That quickly turned into screaming. I stood there quietly because I had no idea what they were saying. I then decided to ask my tour guide, "How long will it take to make a new pendant?" She asked the shop owner. "Twenty minutes." I then said, "How long are we going to be here?" She said, "About 45 minutes." "So, then, we're good." She convinced the shop owner to make a new pendant for me. As I stood there, the man next to me asked, "Where are you from?" I looked at him quizzically and said, "New York." He turned toward his wife and said, "See Louise, I told you she had to be from New York. Only a New Yorker would do that!" That was not the end of the funny. I was the only one who checked my merchandise before I paid for it. Everyone else opened their packages after they already paid and witnessed my altercation. Not one order was right, but they could not do anything about correcting the mistakes. Sometimes it just pays to have that New York state of mind.

After that, we returned to the ship. It was on the late side, and it was time for dinner. None of us had time to shower and change. It did not matter that we were sweaty and dirty. There was so much electricity in the air from all the excitement of the day. There was no lack of dinner conversation as we all shared our adventures of the day.

The following day, the next stop was Israel; and nothing could have prepared me for what I was about to experience. One full day in the holy land. The first stop was Bethlehem and the Church of the Nativity. As I stepped off the bus, I knew deep down this was not just some tourist attraction. I did not know I was stepping into my spiritual awakening. I felt a sense of awe as I entered the church and made my way to the spot marked as Jesus birthplace. I stood where Jesus was born. I was overwhelmed and could feel the tears stream down my face. I never had this feeling in church before. I closed my eyes and needed to take in the moment. I thought to myself, "I wonder if they play Gregorian chant music." Gregorian chant music has always touched me. To me it resonates holiness and being awed by God. I remember standing in the Sistine Chapel in Rome and being awed by the majesty of Michelangelo's masterpiece glorifying God. Then too I thought, "I wonder if they play Gregorian Chant Music." Within seconds, the music was piped into the chapel. Now years later I thought the same thing while standing in the Church of the Nativity. Suddenly, I could not believe what I heard. I opened my eyes: and to my amazement, there were two rows of monks dressed in hooded grey robes with rope belts holding candles singing a Gregorian chant. I was so moved that, instead of tears streaming down my face, I sobbed. This experience is forever burned in my memory.

After that, we traveled by bus to Jerusalem. The first stop was the Via Dolorosa. I could not stop crying. Being Catholic, I would honor the stations of the cross displayed in the church sanctuary. This was another level. I walked through those narrow winding streets in Jerusalem weeping as I followed the path Jesus took as He carried that heavy cross to the hill at Golgotha. I was overcome with the Stations of the Cross positioned along the route. Jesus was becoming more real to me. It was as if Jesus was right there with me.

I tried to hold it together, as I made my way to The Garden of Gethsemane. Somehow, I managed to separate myself from everyone. I stood alone at the Garden. I drank in every tree and blade of grass. As I did, I remember staring at a very funny looking tree. It struck me as strange. Suddenly, I had a vision of Jesus in agony in the garden. He was kneeling with His head bowed down. His hair was wet. He held onto that funny looking tree. I was not one prone to seeing things and I seriously doubted what my eyes beheld. I felt overwhelmed. I felt humbled. I felt small. I felt a weight around me. I did not understand what I experienced, but it felt good. It felt like I was being hugged. How is that possible? Then I heard an audible voice say, "It's simpler than you've been taught." What? Who said that? I looked around. I was alone. Again, "It's simpler than you've been taught." I repeated, "It's simpler than I've been taught. Who? What? I don't understand."

At the Garden of Gethsemane, I had a spiritual experience that changed my life forever. I had a vision of Jesus in agony, and I heard the audible voice of God. I thought I was crazy. I cried for hours, and I did not know why. I just knew that I saw and heard God. He felt so close. He was so real. But instead of focusing on how real He was, I focused on the feeling that I had been lied to my whole life. Because of all the punishment and discipline in Catholic School, I always believed that God was angry with me and so far away. I went to Israel a Catholic; and I came back angry. For four years I did not go to church. That was huge because I was the church every week going to confession kind of Catholic.

As my trip was ending, I had a lot to reflect on. As I reflected, I did not realize this trip would have a profound effect on my life. Even though I left Israel angry, I could not deny what I experienced in Israel. It would not go away. I had some kind of spiritual encounter. They did not teach that in church. They did not teach that in school. I was not afraid. I was touched. It was profound. At that time, I could not wrap my head around it, so, I stored it away. As my trip ended, I just knew that this was the trip of a lifetime. It was now time to return to work. I did not know what was waiting for me. I just knew I was entering a new chapter in my life.

Chapter 3
Rose Colored Glasses

I was on cloud nine. I was refreshed and looked forward to the future. The future came sooner than I expected. When I returned to work, my boss wanted to see me. I did not think anything of it and assumed she wanted to recap what transpired while I was on vacation. I was given a pleasant surprise. She told me that the Assistant Marketing Manager position was now open on the company's flagship business. For two years, I had been the marketing administrator on the nail business: and I was being considered to fill the open spot. She asked if I was interested. Without hesitation, I said "YES!." I was jumping inside. Is it possible that all my hard work would pay off so quickly after receiving my MBA? Focus. She said I needed to meet with the Executive Vice President of Color Cosmetics and the Director of the Nail business, but the position was, basically, mine if I wanted it. I could not wrap my head around that statement. I wanted to say, "You mean I am not competing against anyone else? Is this for real? I met with them that afternoon. I was excited and trepidatious and the same time. I was excited because I knew I would eventually get into marketing. I was trepidatious because the Executive Vice President of Color Cosmetics had a reputation of being difficult to work for. Think Meryl Streep in The Devil Wears Prada.

She was cold, even cruel, and pitted staff members one against the other. There was no room for error. Very few people survived.

In my meeting, The Director told me that they were extremely impressed with my work as the marketing administrator on the nail business. I believed I was doing a good job or why else would I be sitting in this meeting, but it was nice to hear. He said that now that I had my MBA it made perfect sense to offer the Assistant Marketing Manager position to me. Even though my boss clued me in that the position was mine if I wanted it, I was still a bit stunned. I had never been offered a position without an official interview. I was overwhelmed and thanked them for such a great opportunity. The Executive Vice President bluntly told me I would start in two weeks.

I was on my way. All that I had worked toward was starting to unfold. Marketing seemed to be the holy grail. Marketing was the center of the wheel in a company and that excited me. Marketers dealt with everything – business development, marketing strategy, product development, advertising, promotion, and finance. Things were finally falling into place. I would have my finger in every pie, and I savored the prospect of being creative. Even though I knew I would be busy, I felt that I would not have the heavy workload of work and school. I even gave myself license to believe I could add some fun to my life. I was not quite sure how I would fill the new available time in my life; and then there it was. I saw an ad in the newspaper for three free dance lessons at Arthur Murray Dance Studios.

This was like answered prayer. I loved to dance; and I was a frequent patron of disco clubs in New York City. Once a month, my friends and I would travel into the city from Brooklyn and dance the night away. We were not only bridge and tunnel people but oddballs too. We did not live in Manhattan, so we needed to take a bridge or a tunnel to get into the city. And we did not partake of the infamous "party scene" at clubs such as Studio 54. We just danced and enjoyed each other's company.

Dancing was important to me. It was a fun way to exercise, and I was able to express myself. I missed it. When I took ballet as a little girl, I was on toe shoes in six months. I would fantasize about being a famous ballerina. I would be a double threat. I would be an actress and a dancer. When I put my toe shoes on, I was transported into a world of elegance, beauty, and femininity. I would embrace the music and become one with it. My sister also loved to dance. She took modern dance. Where I only fantasized about being a ballerina, my sister had a dream of being a professional dancer. A fantasy and a dream are two very different things. A fantasy is fleeting where a dream is deep within one's soul. Her dream of dancing was as deep as my dream of being an actress. My sister, Deborah, was thirteen and was preparing to audition for the High School of Performing Arts in New York City. It made so much sense. I loved and admired my sister. I looked up to her. I thought she was perfect, especially when she played big sister and protected me. Mostly, I remember my sister as creative. She lit up when she wrote her poetry and short stories. She loved dancing most of all. It gave her so much joy. I remember her beautiful, long legs and how she seemed to move with such grace and elegance. Everything in her came alive. Her creativity shined as she choreographed her audition routine and prepared for weeks for her audition. Then the unthinkable happened. While doing a pivot turn, she dislocated her knee. She was rushed to the hospital. I will never forget coming home from school and my grandmother greeting me at the door. She told me that my sister had an accident. Every emotion rose within me, as I raced up the stairs to see her. She was not there. I then heard the door open, and my mother yelled, "Ma, we're home." I went to the landing of our apartment and watched in horror as my sister was carried up the stairs. She had a cast from hip to toe. Tears filled my eyes. All I could say was, "Sis. Sis." With tears in her eyes, my sister looked at me and said, "Claudia, I'll never dance again." She was devastated. I was so affected by her pain and sadness that I withdrew. I battled deep inside. At the age of ten, I made a life-changing decision. I chose love. I loved my sister so much I could not bear the thought of dancing while she could not. As difficult as it was for me, I gave up ballet. I never put my ballet shoes on again.

Now the thought of dancing again thrilled me. Arthur Murray. Hmmm. The studio was only three blocks from work. I thought, "Why not?" I called and made an appointment to give ballroom and Latin dancing a whirl. When I arrived for my first lesson, I was immediately captivated. Disco had nothing on ballroom and Latin dancing. Besides the dancing, I loved that a man would approach a woman and politely ask, "May I have this dance?" He would escort her to the dance floor and escort her back when the dance was finished. I remember the first-time a man came over and asked me to dance. He extended his arm to escort me to the dance floor. At first, I was hesitant. Then it was as if that adventurous little girl emerged. Just as I had started escaping into my own little world at four years old, I allowed myself to, once again, create a character for myself and play out my story in my head. As I took his arm, I saw myself as a woman floating across the dance floor and enjoying every minute of it. I even saw myself as beautiful. I imagined that we talked and laughed as we twirled around the dance floor. We enjoyed each other. We were one with the music. The one difference was this was real. I was dancing with a man. Unfortunately, the reality did not quite fulfill the fantasy. I was a bit timid and concerned about making a mistake. I often broke the cardinal rule of not looking down. Experience would teach me that looking up would allow me to follow the man's lead. To follow, I needed to give up control. At first that was challenging. I needed to trust him. As we started to dance, the timidity began to leave. I allowed him to lead me across the dance floor. It was like nothing I had experienced before. I did not want this feeling to end. When the music finished, he escorted me back. For a moment in time, I got to feel like a woman. How civil. How respectful. How lovely.

As I waited for my lesson to begin, I could not take my eyes off the teachers and students in the main ballroom. I could tell the beginners from those who had more experience. I looked forward to my lesson, but I was a bit nervous and a bit timid. This was a new world. My teacher came over and introduced himself. He was Latin with dark, thick hair. He started to ask me about any dance experience I might have had. I told I did ballet as a kid, and I danced disco. He thought for a moment and said, "Let's start with a waltz."

I now entered the world of being in a man's arms. I knew I would be safe, but I was uncomfortable. That discomfort soon started to fade away. My first lesson turned into another and another and another. I danced for twelve years and enjoyed every minute of it. I even competed proAm. I was the Am. I enjoyed it so much I got carried away. I invested in a dance costume designed just for me. I did not recognize myself in this costume that doubled as a ballroom dress with a flowing removeable skirt which transformed into a sexy Latin dress. I looked sexy. I looked like a woman, but I felt uncomfortable in my own skin. I was playing a part. And I did it well. In competition, I won award after award. As a dancer I blossomed. Instead of discos, I now went out to the Rainbow Room in Rockefeller Center with a group of friends I made through the dance studio. We would save up for six months, get all dressed up and dine and dance until dawn. The first time we went to the Rainbow Room, we spent our reserved dinner seating dancing and never ordered dinner. We went out later for pizza. After that, we booked our reservations for the entire evening, not just for one dinner seating. Since we took up three dinner seatings, we tipped very well. We also hit such famous dance halls as Roseland in Times Square and The Cat Club. This was the creative outlet I needed because I soon learned that marketing was not what I expected it to be. And, sadly, my personal life and free time became nonexistent.

I was an Assistant Marketing Manager for one week when my director came into my office and closed the door. He announced that he had resigned. I was stunned. I did not see that coming at all. I said, "Excuse me, did you know this was coming when I started last week?" He said he did, but it was too soon to say anything. My head was spinning. I then asked, "Who will I be reporting to?" GULP!

The next morning, I met with my new boss, the Executive Vice President of Color Cosmetics. I trembled. She told me that she would have a status meeting with me once a week. I just looked at her in disbelief. "Once a week? We are working on the biggest relaunch in the company's history. Shouldn't we meet more often?" She snapped at me. "I don't have time. Figure it out!" As the shock wore off, she looked at me and said she needed me to pull a report together on the new sales projections. She needed the report that night. My heart sank. I had made plans for that night. As my new life began, so did the possibility of a romance. I had been introduced to a man who just fit the bill. He was European, handsome, educated, refined and when he opened his mouth to speak, my heart skipped a beat as his words lilted with a silky Spanish accent. He invited me to a concert to see Segovia. I just adore classical Spanish guitar music. I was over the moon. We seemed to have so much in common. I sheepishly looked at my boss and told her I had plans that night. I was given the death stare which sent chills through me. She said, "What did I just say!?!" My fear of authority caused my wall to loom large. I caved. I headed back to my small office. I paced. I did not want to call the man of my dreams and tell him I needed to cancel. I beat myself up. Why can't I ever do what I want to do? I finally picked up the phone and called him. I told him I had to work late that night. I apologized for the short notice. Before I could utter another word, he hung up on me. The slam was so loud I jolted the phone from my ear. I just stood there and stared at the phone. Deep inside I knew I would never hear from him again. That was a defining moment. I made my choice that work would come first, and my personal life would play second fiddle to that.

Begrudgingly, I did that report. Her words "figure it out" rang in my head. Figure it out I did. I soon realized that I was still a marketing administrator with an Assistant Marketing Manager title. Thankfully, I knew how to get things done. I was expected to do everything on the business. No one guided me or taught me the marketing ropes. I worked around the clock and made it happen. I was angry and frustrated. I also felt I was taken advantage of. After six months, I felt I should be rewarded for my hard work. I got up the courage to meet with the Executive Vice President and ask for a promotion. I laid out my case, and to my surprise, she agreed to elevate me to Marketing Manager on the nail business. I did not know whether to laugh or cry. I finally stood up for myself. In the joy, was the pang that standing up for myself came a little late. Being promoted was bittersweet. It would have tasted better if I could have shared my news with the man I let go of for the job. It was a biting reminder that the job came first. I wanted to have fun. I wanted to be the little girl playing with her mobile again where laughter filled every part of me. Instead, I resigned myself to the fact that, as an adult, I could not have fun either in my life or on the job. Everything was work. I needed to let go of these thoughts and focus on another good thing came out of that meeting. The Executive VP decided to consolidate the nail business under the direction of the Director of Lip. I now had an intermediary between myself and the Executive VP, and I would finally get some needed marketing direction. I did learn some things: but I was just a body leaning on people to get things done.

The longer I stayed in marketing the more I realized I did not fit in. Marketing types tend to be competitive both on the job and in the marketplace. I did not have the personality to play politics or office games. I tend to be an observer. I like to take in the lay of the land before I form an opinion. Not so with marketers. My experience showed me that they, generally, like to be heard and often. They tend to jump right in and offer their opinions without fully assessing the facts and situations. Because of my approach to my work, I receded into the background, and I naively believed doing the job with excellence is what got rewarded. The more competitive things became on the job, the more I retreated into being an introvert. That reaction became blood in the water, and I became a target. I did not know how to navigate the waters. I knew this was happening, and I did not know how to deal with it. I wanted to scream, "Look at me. Hear me!" Instead, I became that little girl who hid in closets. I not only hid my voice but also my anger and frustration.

However, there were times I could not stuff my frustration anymore and my temper would flare. I remember a time when I chaired a meeting on promotional materials for the launch of the nail business. Present at the meeting was the Executive Vice President of Marketing. She liked to push buttons. As I led the meeting, suddenly she started to take over and started talking business strategy. That was not the focus of the meeting, and within a short time, the meeting went off the rails. Because she was who she was, those in attendance shifted with her and were out of their depth. She pushed my buttons and challenged me on the strategy of the relaunch in a promotional meeting. I could not believe what I said to her. "The strategy for the relaunch has been approved and this is a promotional meeting based on that strategy. Let us stay focused on the purpose of this meeting." She just looked at me and did not say anything. I got the meeting back on track and everyone had their marching orders. I left the meeting and headed back to my office. My fear of being punished caused my wall to grow larger right in front of me. I couldn't stop thinking "I'm going to get fired. I'm going to get fired." I did not get fired. She liked the way I stood up to her. Unfortunately, I needed to be brought to a boiling point to do that.

I decided I needed a change. As I reflected on my career, I felt what I was doing was not real marketing. I knew I needed to be trained. I did not want to just be a body leaning on people to get things done. I searched for a new job, and I resigned after I accepted a position as an Assistant Marketing Manager at Lever Brother. Even though I took a step back in title, I felt I was going to be involved in true consumer product marketing and doors would open for me. My cosmetics/beauty background was a plus since my new position was on the new Dove skin care product line. I found myself involved in marketing research, new product development and marketing strategy and planning. I tended to gravitate toward the more creative elements of marketing, namely new product development and advertising. I lacked the more analytical side of the business, which unfortunately, was the lion's share of an assistant's job responsibility. I had a good working relationship with my Marketing Director, and she helped train me in the analytics of the business. Even though my director had patience and I had an attitude to learn, I struggled with the analytics. I felt that no matter how much I tried I would never get it. I felt it was a major weakness that was noticed. I felt that I was once again being called up in front of the class and being humiliated that I was failing in math.

As time went on, I began to feel even more insecure. I worked so hard to get my MBA and get into marketing; but now I was in the pool of Assistant Marketing Managers who attended ivy league schools such as Wharton and Harvard. I went to Pace. At that time, not exactly ivy league. They had so much confidence, and once again, I felt that I was not good enough. The one thing I did have was common sense. This was a challenge for me when I needed to take direction from management that I felt flew in the face of common sense. This would play against me.

I was with Lever Brothers about a year when it was announced that the company had purchased Chesebrough-Pond's in 1987. Since I was in the personal products division, we were relocated to the Chesebrough-Pond's headquarters in Greenwich, Connecticut. This was a stressful time in that I needed to sell my co-op in Brooklyn, find a place to live in Connecticut and settle in at work. Then more stress was added. I was out on a Saturday night with a friend in Brooklyn. It was pouring rain and I slowed my car down to stop for a light that was changing to red. The driver in the car coming in the opposite direction decided to race through the yellow light and skidded out of control on the wet pavement and hit my car head on. Even though everything moved in slow motion, I heard myself say, "Is this really happening. Why me?" Coming out of the slow motion, I realized my car was pushed about twenty feet into a bus stop. I could not move. We waited for the police and the ambulance to arrive. Instead of having an evening of fun with a good friend, my Saturday night was spent in the emergency room at Coney Island Hospital. When I left the hospital, I was in a neck brace and in so much pain. I now struggled not only emotionally but physically. Yet, somehow, I needed to dig deep and forget the pain and forge ahead. I needed to make a good impression with my new management. I could not appear weak. More importantly, I could not let them know I was weak.

Through it all, I managed to find and purchase a condominium near the beach in Stamford, Connecticut which was about 15 minutes from work. This was such pleasant change from taking the 1 & 1/2 hour subway ride from Brooklyn to Manhattan every day and then back home again at night. Instead of skyscrapers, I was now surrounded by trees and the posh setting of Greenwich.

While I settled in, I saw a chiropractor for three months to get my neck and back aligned again. I started to see light at the end of the tunnel. The pain dissipated, and I gained better focus and adapted to the changes in my life. I am always amazed at the tenacity and resolve I have to get through circumstances.

I soon realized that the period of adjustment with the relocation was not only for me, but for those relocating and for those already at Chesebrough-Pond's. The companies needed to be merged. As I started to come out from under, history repeated itself. My new boss, resigned about a month after I started working with him. He originally worked at Lever Brothers and resigned to work at Chesebrough-Pond's. Now he was faced with working with the same management team he left. I could not believe it. I needed to digest this and wondered, "Why does this keep happening to me?" I needed to feel settled. I needed to feel some sense of security. That was not to be. I was moved to another brand working on Dimension hair care and Rave Perm Products. Dimension was on its way out and I had to manage the closeout. I became known as the Queen of Distress Merchandising. This was not exactly a title that I aspired to, but all my years of marketing administration played a hand in the process. As for the Rave brand, I now reported to a newly promoted Marketing Manager who was an ivy leaguer who jockeyed for position. We seemed to work well together, even though I felt uncomfortable around her.

We were relaunching the Rave Perm Hair Care product line. I permed my own hair to make sure I understood how it all worked. Giving myself a perm gave me a flashback to when I was a little girl. My mother could not accept that I had straight hair. Her hair was naturally curly, and my sister took after her. The only curl I had was a cowlick that caused my hair to stick out on the right side of my head. It looked like I could perch a bird on it. My mother decided to cart me off to the Little Princess Shop to get a perm. I did not want a perm. I sat there with rods in my hair, and I was attached to a weird machine. It looked like I was being electrocuted. When the rods came out, I looked like a frizz head. I cried all the way home. I did not want anyone to see me. I hid in my room. I did not want to go to school. I did not want to go anywhere. After three days, my mother could not take it anymore. She carted me back to The Little Princess Shop and had the stylist, or beautician in those days, cut my hair short. That image burned in my memory as I was the true marketer and tried my own product. I went from short straight hair to short curly hair overnight. Thankfully, history did not repeat itself. I did not look like a frizz head. Since my hair was short, it grew out quickly. As for the Rave products, we spent months working on the relaunch and now it was time to present the new brand at the sales meeting. The sales presentation ignited a spark in me.

We decided to do the presentation like a film noir spy story with detectives looking for the perfect perm. I played different characters during the presentation. I took to it like a duck takes to water. I immersed myself in each character and had a blast sharing the facts about the product launch. Many people, including management, told my boss how much they enjoyed the presentation, especially my performance.

What surprised me is that I just went with it. I was not nervous at all. It felt right.

After that I was switched over to another brand, namely toothpaste. I now reported to a different Marketing Manager. I started to notice that I was getting switched around at the same level while other assistants were being promoted to associates. My self-confidence was shaky. I felt rejected and that I was not good enough to be promoted. I did do my job well, but I did not know how to play the game. Then, a new manager was brought in from England to oversee the brand. He played the game well and, he too, jockeyed for position. He made sure he was in the right place and the right time. I receded into the background. A new Director from England was also brought in to oversee the oral care division. I felt I was back at square one. Things went from bad to worse. The Director and I did not hit it off at all. He unnerved me. To me, he had black eyes and a black heart. He smelled blood in the water with me and he went in for the kill. Assistants had cubicles, and our cubicles were next to each other. The Director would visit the assistant next to me and praise her work. He made sure I could hear the accolades. For me, nothing but ridicule and disdain. I could not seem to do anything right.

The most glaring faux pax on my part was my common sense. He did not appreciate it. I worked on developing a new toothpaste brand and we were in the market research stage. The Director had another pet project that he wanted to see launched instead of my project. In a nutshell, the market research was favorable with my project and not the Director's. It made sense to me to recommend pursuing my brand. The Director dug his heels in and did what he could to analyze the market research to favor his project. Day after day, he shot me down not only privately but in front of others. Instead of being confident, I withdrew and succumbed to his taunting.

Early one morning, I was summoned to the Director's office. He matter-of-factly told me, "I'm laying you off." I do not think I even heard what he said. "Excuse me?" Again, "I'm laying you off. You just don't fit in here." As he said it, there seemed to be this sick sense of glee as his words spilled from his mouth and landed on my ears. All I could do was squeak out, "But, my business is up." That fell on deaf ears.

After he did what he set out to do, he got up and ushered me into the Vice President's office. I think I was in shock, but I distinctly remember him bluntly saying to me, "You really should think about another line of work."

My head was spinning. "How could I be laid off. People with my work ethic do not get laid off." I felt like such a failure and my confidence was low. In my mind I kept replaying, "You should think about another line of work." I worked so hard to get into marketing. I could not even think straight. I was so broken. There was one bright spot that showed I was good at my job. After I was laid off, a friend of mine at the company called me. The results of a major promotion I initiated came in. I stood alone with this promotion. No one supported it, especially the director. My friend told me they were all in a meeting when the market share numbers were revealed. The promotion I developed and brought to market was a huge success. The numbers dwarfed every other product in the market. There was only one explanation, and it could not be dismissed. My promotion worked. I saw what no one else did. Even though it vindicated me, I could not relish the success. I was out of a job and had to face the reality of finding work.

I was sent to outplacement to help me work through the layoff. Unfortunately, the damage was done. My confidence was shattered. Who was going to hire such a failure? I took the first job that came my way. I went to work at the Regina Company which manufactured vacuum cleaners. The company was coming out of bankruptcy. I got up at the crack of dawn to drive 125 miles a day from Stamford, Connecticut to Rahway, New Jersey in bumper-to-bumper traffic. The company was in a rundown warehouse across the street from a maximum-security prison. It was as if this was a symbol of my life and my career. I felt my career was going nowhere. I felt my life was going nowhere. I felt like I was in prison. And twice a day the roaring blast of security sirens would not only shake the atmosphere but shake me to my core. What was I doing? Working at the company, I felt like I worked on the island of misfit toys. All of us were out of work through layoffs or corporate mergers. It was a bad situation, and it quickly became clear that there was no way to turn this company around. There was a round of layoffs. I was spared, but I had to lay off my assistant. Things continued to go downhill, and the company could not make its way out of bankruptcy. Within eight months, I was out of work again.

I had a short stint working for a local publishing company and then I worked for an executive recruiter during a major recession. Who does that? I could not find a job for myself and now I tried to find work for others when jobs were few and far between. Somehow as I broke away from corporate, I think, deep down, I had a flicker that I had to stop doing things the same way. I needed to look at things differently. That flicker faded fast. Things were not going well. I felt I was making one bad decision after another. I felt lost and I struggled to figure out where I fit in and what to do next.

Chapter 4

A Desperate Cry

I was in such a desperate place. I continued to look at things the way I always did. My life centered around my work and being successful. I lived for the world's definition of success which meant being promoted and climbing the corporate ladder. I was not even close. I did not know where to turn. I felt I made one bad decision after another. The failure I felt was difficult for me on another level because I was the only one in my family who was ever let go from a job. We did not get fired. I found it hard to face my family even though they seemed supportive. I remember it was Christmas; and because I was financially strapped, I only bought a Christmas gift for my niece who was six years old at the time. After I gave her the gift, she pulled me aside; and in her innocent sweet way, she said, "Aunt Claudia, I know you don't have a job. You do not need to give me a Christmas gift. It's okay." In that moment, I had a flood of emotion. I just wanted to hug my niece, but I was hit with the reality that the only way she could have known I was out of work was if she overheard my sister and brother-in-law discussing my situation. My mind raced with the horrific thought that they must have been talking about me, and what they said was not good. They must have discussed that I was a failure. Why else would my niece want to give back the Christmas gift I gave to her. I had to fight back tears. I was brought to rock bottom, and I did the only thing left I knew to do. I cried out to God.

Two years earlier I started searching for God. It had been four years since I walked away from the Catholic Church after my trip to Israel. I decided to try again. I went back to the Catholic Church. No, that was not it. I tried a Presbyterian Church. No. A Methodist Church. No. Then I decided I did not want religion. Instead of being a comfort, for me, religion was like a prison. For me, religion meant punishment. I had the thought that I studied catechism in Catholic school. There were scriptures in the catechism books. Maybe I should study the bible. I never studied the bible. I threw the prison doors wide open and attended a non-denominational evangelical congregational church in Stamford, Connecticut. I was not quite sure what that meant. I just knew it was non-denominational. As I attended bible studies, I struggled to understand the need to ask Jesus into my heart to be saved. As a Catholic, I learned it was all about work. I rationalized that I was a good a person. I did not murder anyone. I did not steal anything. How could it be as simple as asking Jesus into my heart? I became consumed with answering that burning question.

I needed to find a job; but all I could do was read the bible. I devoured it. The Word started to come to life in me; and it is when I read Ephesians 2:8-9 (KJV) that I had my AHA moment. "For by grace are ye saved through faith; and that not of yourselves: it is the gift of God: Not of works, lest any man should boast." On January 21, 1991, I curled up in a fetal position on my bedroom floor. Clutching my bible, I cried out "Jesus help me." That is not the traditional sinner's prayer, but that is all I knew to do at that time. After doing that, I began to have a strong desire to pray. I prayed about everything and everyone. What struck me as strange was my need to pray for Hollywood. It would take 11 years for me to understand why.

That night I was awakened at 2:00 in the morning. I opened my eyes and was alarmed to see two demons hovering over me. They were hideous with dark brown, shell-like skin, bulging eyes and fangs for teeth. It felt like I was in the middle of some horror movie. They taunted me. Poked at me. I wanted to scream, but I could not. I was frightened to my very core. I did not know what to do. I was shaking. All I could manage to say was, "Jesus help me." I had said that just a few hours earlier when I asked Him into my heart. Suddenly, two huge angels appeared in my bedroom. They were white and glittering. A glow of light surrounded them. Simultaneously, they both lifted their left arms and motioned for the demons to leave. They immediately disappeared. Such a peace came over me. I felt safe and protected. I fell off to sleep as if nothing happened. I have been seeing angels ever since.

The following day after I asked Jesus into my heart, I was almost killed on Interstate 95 as I was returning home from a job interview. It was dusk and about 20 degrees below zero. I was driving south in the left lane at about sixty-five miles an hour, when my car jolted forward and started to stall. I miraculously made it over three lanes to get out at the exit in Bridgeport. My car seemed to only go in reverse. I made it down the exit ramp, and I saw police cars. In reverse, I made it to where the police were stationed. They immediately came over to my car and said I had to get out there. There was a police raid in progress in a drug house. I was shaking. I told the officers what happened to my car and that it would only drive in reverse. One officer called a tow truck and stayed with me for protection. I was towed to a Sears automotive shop. After about an hour wait, I was told that my transmission had exploded and that I was lucky to be alive. I was conflicted. I just asked Jesus into my heart, and I was almost killed on the freeway. I did what I usually did. I looked at the glass half empty. The key words were "I was lucky to be alive." I did not see that the hand of God protected me. I broke down. I called a cab and was able to get home. I dealt with the car the next day.

The water that remained in my half empty glass drained quickly. I was now faced with the stress of not knowing how I was going to pay for my car. I did not know where the money was going to come from to pay my mortgage. Yet, all I could do was read the bible and spend time with the Lord. It was at this time that I began to see that luck had nothing to do with it. Miraculously, money came in to help me pay my bills. I received an unexpected tax refund and insurance claim payment. I was grateful, but I was not in a place to recognize that the Lord was my Provider.

My stress level was high. It was during this time that I needed to find an inexpensive way to do something to get my mind off my circumstances. I saw an ad in the local paper that the Community Theatre offered acting classes. I thought about it for a nano second. I quickly decided why not? It was just what I needed. Except for drama classes in high school, I never studied acting. I did not know what to expect. What I found challenging was that I was so corporate that I could not wrap my head around letting go and being another character. I resisted exercises to release a freedom. I remember my acting teacher called me up and asked me to play Martha from Who's Afraid of Virginia Wolf singing I am a Little Teapot. I thought he was crazy. I just stood there and looked at him. He snapped, "Do it!" I got jolted and I took a deep breath. I started to squeak out I am a Little Teapot. Suddenly, a strange freedom started to take over. I felt myself starting to absorb the character of Martha. I took on such an attitude while singing the song. I started to live in the moment. I started to understand taking direction. For a brief moment, I started to let go. For a brief moment, I started to have fun.

I wanted more than a brief moment. Then, to my surprise, I saw an ad in the local paper that the Community Theater was holding auditions for Who's Afraid of Virginia Wolf. Was this a sign? I decided to schedule an audition. I had no idea what I was doing; but I familiarized myself with the audition scene and just went for it. I did not put any pressure on myself because I just went for the experience of auditioning. I was also wearing a knee brace which was very noticeable. I had dislocated my right knee playing volleyball. I jumped up to spike the ball over the net. As I did, I heard a loud pop in my knee. That spike won the point, and I looked so good as I went down. So, I thought, besides having no acting experience, no one is going to cast me with that big, glaring knee brace on my knee. A week later my phone rang, and it was the Director of the play. We chatted and then he said, "I just wanted to call and tell you that I really enjoyed your audition. I do need to cast someone with more experience, but you did a great job." I was overwhelmed. I was surprised he did not even mention my knee brace. He just talked about my audition. I could not hold back my excitement. I told him, "Thank you. That means so much. I have never auditioned for anything before." There was a pregnant pause. He then said, "You're kidding." Me, "No, I'm not." Then the kicker, "I'm going to give you one piece of advice."

"Do not quit acting. Do not ever quit acting."

His words hit me as I hung up the phone. At first, I lingered on his praise that I did such a good job. It had been a long time since anyone said those words to me. Then, I focused on his parting words. Do not quit acting. Do not ever quit acting. As much as everything in me was jumping that acting could be a possibility in my life, all I could hear were my mother's words so long ago. "Acting is not responsible.

Acting does not put food on the table. Acting is not a real job." My excitement quickly faded. Reality kicked in. Once again, I buried the thought of acting. I needed to be responsible. I needed to get a real job.

As daunting as getting a real job was, I continued to study the Word of God. Since I wanted to be obedient to the Lord, eight months after I said Jesus help me, I was baptized. It was an interesting day. My dad had called me the day before and asked what I was doing on Sunday. I told him I had plans. He asked what they were. I hesitated. My dad was an agnostic and my mother was so Catholic. I thought they would not understand. I finally said I was going to be baptized. After a deafening silence, he asked me, "Is this important to you." I said, "Yes." In typical dad fashion, he said, "You're Mom and I will be there." I could not believe what I heard. I said, "You will?" He then said, "Your mother and I have never missed an important thing in your life. We're not going to start now." I started to cry. They were there front and center. My mom was stone faced. That look reminded me of the scowl she used to have on her face when she was disappointed in me. I knew she did not want to be there. When my sister and I left the Catholic Church, my mother went to confession and confessed that she was a failure as a mother. The priest asked her to explain. She told him that both her daughters left the church. He thought we were out there living foot loose and fancy free. He was surprised when my mother told him they were doing this born-again thing. He confirmed that my sister and I were both following the Lord. Thankfully, in wisdom, he told my mother that we serve the same God. He told her she should be grateful that we had not left our faith. As for my dad, he took it all in. After service, I introduced them to my pastor. We then went out for brunch. Even though it was August, there was an icy chill in the air. We talked about everything but the service and my baptism. It never came up again.

I continued to seek the Lord and it was now spring. It was a beautiful day in May. I had my windows open and enjoyed the fresh air. I was in my living room and on my knees praying. That was how I was taught to pray, so that is what I did. I had such a childlike faith. I remember putting my head down on my sofa and softly saying, "Jesus, I love you." Suddenly, it felt like arms wrapped around me and gave me a big hug. In a split second, I felt comforted and loved. Was that Jesus? Unexpectedly, I was flung to the floor and started shaking. It happened so fast I did not have any time to resist. I had never experienced anything like this before. It was as if I was present, but I was not. For some reason, I did not have any fear. I did not have any idea what was happening to me, but I just went with it. After almost two hours, I opened my eyes and managed to get up. Then, the strangest thing happened. Without even thinking about speaking, words just started pouring out of me. As the words continued, I realized I was talking funny. I had no idea what I was saying. Again, I just went with it. Surprisingly, I was not freaked out. I had such a peace. Somehow, I just knew it was from God.

Later that day, I called my sister. She had received the Lord the year before. I was open with her and told her what happened. She listened, and then, in her calm way, she explained that I had received the baptism of the Holy Spirit with the evidence of speaking in tongues. The what? She told me she had not received this gift, but it was scriptural. She pointed out where I could find it in scripture and suggested I speak with my pastor. That made sense, but I never saw anything like that happening in church before. I started thinking of every excuse I could not to meet with him. What if he thinks I am crazy? He is only a temporary pastor. At that time, our church was going through transition. Our pastor had moved back to Wisconsin with his family. The interim pastor did not know me. Facing authority was difficult enough without adding another layer of discomfort to the mix. Deep down, I knew my sister was right, and I sheepishly made an appointment.

When we met, I introduced myself and told him what I had experienced. I expected some discussion or some sage wisdom. Instead, what he said shocked me to the core. He said, "You need to be careful. This is from the devil." I just looked at him as I got that knot in the pit of my stomach. I did not know what to say. I thought, "Am I possessed by the devil? I physically felt a weight on me. It was the same weight I felt at the Garden of Gethsemane. What came next had to be the Holy Spirit. I was not the type to challenge authority. I felt they knew more than me. Instead, what came out of my mouth was, "If it is from the devil, why do I want to pray more?" He just looked at me. It was as if, in that moment, I was no longer a little girl cowering to authority. I think, in that moment, I took a hammer and took a swat at my wall. Without realizing it, in that moment, I took a step forward.

That moment of stepping forward was brief. I left more confused than when I went to meet with him. I did not know what to do. I felt like, now, I did not fit into church either. I just wanted confirmation that I was not crazy, and I needed a sense of belonging. The one thing I knew was that I had a spiritual experience. I could not deny it. Yet, I believed others knew more than me. I was screaming inside. God just show me what to do! Who am I? Is there something wrong with me? Why do I think differently than everyone else? Why does it seem like I just know what I know; yet I feel I am wrong at the same time? I want to fit in, but I do not. I was conflicted. I thought churches welcomed everybody. It was here that I had the painful realization that churches push people away if they do not fit into their neat little box.

Validation was more important than fitting into their box. I decided to take another approach. I was friendly with an elder in the church. As a new believer, she had taken me under her wing. She knew I was not a crazy person. Deep inside, I knew I was not a crazy person. She met with me, and I told her about what I had experienced and what the pastor said to me. She sat quietly and listened. Thankfully, she was not judgmental. When I finished telling her of my experience, she explained that the church did not believe in this. She did say that other churches do. How is it possible that there is one bible, and each denomination believes different things? That did not make any sense to me. It felt like church was trying to squeeze God into what they believed instead of the other way around. She suggested that I speak with one of the pastoral candidates who was interviewing for the open pastor's job. This would be worse than speaking to the interim pastor. At least the interim pastor saw me in church and in bible studies. This pastoral candidate did not know me at all. I took a deep breath and called to make an appointment to speak by phone. I explained that I was referred to him by the elder in the church. We spoke for an hour. He asked some specific questions like what does the language sound like? I said, "It's kind of melodic. It sounds like Italian." As a note, I do not speak Italian or any other language. He listened intently and said he wanted to make sure this was truly from the Holy Spirit. He said, if it were demonic, it would sound dark and ugly. He advised that I seek out an Assembly of God Church. He explained they believe in the gifts of the Spirt. I thanked him for taking the time to speak with me. As a side note, he did not get the pastoral position. His thinking was a little too radical for them.

His advice resonated with me, and I did what he suggested. I found an Assembly of God Church in Stamford, CT. It was a bizarre experience. During worship, I witnessed people raising their hands and singing in the spirit. They, too, were talking funny. Then, someone got up and gave a prophetic word from the Lord. I must have had a look of disbelief on my face. I looked up and asked, "Lord, where do you have me now?" This would be a running theme throughout my walk with the Lord. As uncomfortable as I was, I realized that what I had been experiencing, they were doing.

As submissive as I was to authority, I was hit with the painful realization that I entered new territory. I could no longer rely on the crutches that I established in my life. I could no longer rely on myself. I needed to make the choice to go through the pain of dying to myself. With childlike faith and determination, I searched for the truth. I entered into the School of The Holy Spirit. I put one foot in front of the other and asked the Lord to guide and teach me. He answered my prayers. I learned that I was not alone. There were people like me who had spiritual encounters with the Lord. As I entered this new territory, I was nervous. But I had to know more. I had to keep moving forward.

It was now July, and I was in such a desperate financial place. In the last minute, the Lord came through. Out of the blue, I received a phone call from an executive recruiter that I had worked with in the past. He said he had a wonderful job opportunity for a Senior Marketing Manager on the flagship business of a major cosmetics company. I perked up and wanted to know more. As we chatted about the opportunity, I asked him, "What company?"

He said, "Maybelline." Dead silence. I then croaked out, "Aren't they in Memphis?"

After I got over the shock of the possibility of leaving Connecticut to live in Memphis, I agreed to interview with the company. I must confess I was nervous. My track record of working in corporate was painful. As I flew to Memphis, I fought the urge to cut and run. My past experiences with layoffs and takeovers loomed large. I did not want to repeat the past. I arrived for my interview, and I met with Human

Resources and my potential boss. We hit it off, and surprisingly, I did not have a knot in my stomach. They were warm and approachable. We talked and got to know each other a bit. I started to breathe a little. I was, then, given the realtor's grand tour of Memphis living and housing possibilities. I needed to be picked up off the floor. Three-bedroom, two bath houses were cheaper than my one-bedroom condominium in Connecticut. I had a lot to digest. As I flew back to Connecticut, I kept thinking about my visit to Memphis. Was I ready to leave?

I never lived outside the tri-state area. I never lived far away from my parents. One thing I knew, I was very much a New Yorker. New York was my home. New York had so much to offer. Then the reality hit that New York was not offering work. I liked Elvis, but would I be happy in Memphis? I needed to be sure.

The following day I received a phone call from the recruiter. He wanted my take on things. I told him I went from putting Memphis first to putting Maybelline first in analyzing the opportunity. I liked what I heard and what I saw. He quickly confirmed that they wanted to pursue another meeting with me. The next time I would meet with six other people in the company from colleagues and subordinates to support teams. Having people respect and work well together was part of the culture at Maybelline. It was an important part of the interviewing process. This made complete sense to me; and we arranged for my next visit to Maybelline.

I can honestly say I never enjoyed interviewing as much as I did that day. I felt so comfortable, and I was able to have open and honest conversations with everyone I met. What struck me the most was that these were "real" people. Even though this was still the beauty industry, they did not portray the high-brow persona of New York. They were educated but down to earth. Interestingly, they were like me. I was intrigued that many of the people who worked at the company moved to Memphis to specifically work for Maybelline. The company had such a good reputation and lived up to it. I did not want to make the same mistake I did when I took the first job that came along after I was laid off. This felt different. This felt right.

I had a long delay flying back to New York and did not arrive home until about 3:00 in the morning. I was exhausted. Apparently, the HR Director was in early contact with my recruiter wanting to offer me the position; and he had been trying to reach me. I finally got the message and returned the call. We went through all the specifics of the offer; and one major specific jumped out at me. They offered me more money than I asked for. Was this a sign? I put aside all the doubt and pain of the past. I went with the feeling that this felt right. I said, "Yes."

I was genuinely excited. I now needed to share the good news with my parents. This was not going to be easy. My mother had just come through triple bypass surgery. Having me close by was a comfort to her. I called and told them I was driving down for a visit. This was outside of my structured visit every two weeks from Connecticut. I showed up with some sparkling apple cider. Since I do not drink, I was not about to splurge on champagne. I arrived at my parents' home. My mother was sitting in the kitchen. She was tired but recovering well from the surgery. As I went over to give her a kiss, she looked at me and said, "You found a job." A mother just knows. I looked at her, and said, "Yes, Mom, I did." Then, she said, "You're leaving New York." It was not a question. It was a statement. I just looked at her as if to say, "How did you know?" I told her I received a wonderful offer from Maybelline, and the company was in Memphis. She got a panged look on her face, but she knew I had to go. I explained to my parents that I was only a two-hour plane ride away. At that time, Northwest airlines had its hub in Memphis. It would take as long to fly from Memphis to New York as it does to get from Connecticut into New York City in traffic. We toasted my new job. I did not realize how leaving New York was another small step forward in coming out from under my parents' wing. It was scary.

The hard part was over. I now had to figure out the logistics of moving from Connecticut to Memphis. They wanted me on board by the end of August. That gave me one month to pull things together. I decided to test the waters and put my condo on the market while I readied myself for the big move. My plan was to purchase a home in Memphis with the proceeds from the sale of my condominium. I quickly learned that was not going to happen. The real estate market had collapsed in 1992 and my condominium was under water. After the shock wore off, I took a very business-like approach to handling the disappointing news. I decided to rent out my condominium and hire a rental manager to oversee the property and find an appropriate tenant.

My thought was to sell the condominium when the real estate market improved. With that plan squared away, I packed up my car and drove three days from Stamford, Connecticut to Memphis, Tennessee. The whole drive down I kept thinking, "Am I doing the right thing? Am I going to fit it?" A New Yorker in Memphis, Oy Vey!

I started out on my three-day drive to Memphis. Except for my concern about fitting in, it was an uneventful journey. That changed while I drove from East Tennessee to Memphis. It was beautiful day, and the sky was clear blue with not a cloud to be seen. I listened to worship music, and I looked up to the sky. There right before my eyes were clouds in the perfect form of a cross. I could not take my eyes off it. My eyes were wide, and my mouth dropped open as I beheld the cross. I believe that was a sign from God that He was with me. That cross was clearly in my view for about thirty miles before it started to dissipate. As a new believer making some dramatic changes in my life, this sign was truly a comfort. Since I was driving, I tried hard to keep my emotions in check. The last thing I needed was to be involved in an accident. With a lump in my throat, I verbally thanked God for the confirmation that I was, indeed, doing the right thing.

I arrived safely in Memphis on a Sunday afternoon. I was in town for about ten minutes when my concern about fitting in hit me right in the face. I looked at my oil gauge, and it seemed to indicate that I needed oil. I found a gas station and discovered they were not able to check my oil. It was about one hundred degrees and 100% humidity outside. I sat in my air-conditioned car while I flipped through the owner's manual to see how I could check my oil level. According to the manual, I needed to check the dipstick. I did not even know what a dipstick was. All I ever did was put gas in my car and turn on the ignition. I left the other maintenance details to the mechanic. With my trusty owner's manual in hand, I popped the hood, got out of the car, and braved the overwhelming heat and humidity. I was ready to check my oil. Suddenly, this red pickup truck appeared out of nowhere and stopped next to my car. I was startled. This man, I will call him Beau, got out of the truck. He had long stringy hair, a straggly beard and he wore a sweaty bandana on his head. I was convinced he had a sawed-off shotgun in his truck and my life was hanging in the balance. He approached me. I did not know what to do. Was this a moment of fight or flight? He towered over me. Forget fight! Every stereotypical thought raced through my mind. Is he a convict? Is he going to kill me? Where are the police? Should I scream? I stood frozen.

He started to speak. "Scuse me, Ma'am, y'all need some help?" My independent, get out of my space New York came through. With a shaky voice, I said, "No, just checking the oil. Looking for the dipstick." To my surprise, he said, "Little lady like you shouldn't be doin' that. Let me." He leaned in under the hood; and without any hesitation, pulled out the dipstick. He held it with this really dirty rag and showed it to me, as if I knew what I was looking at. He said, "No Ma'm, your oil's just fine." I looked up and with disbelief croaked out, "Thank you." "Beau" then said, "You don't sound like you're from round here." My mind started to race. Do I dare tell him I am from New York? That makes me a Yankee. I skirted the issue and said, "I just moved to town." With such glee, he said, "Well, I sure do hope you like your time in Memphis." I was stunned. Not only was a stranger helping me, he, actually, seemed to care about my situation. As this realization hit me, my tough New York attitude dissolved. I said, "If everyone is as nice as you, I think I'm going to love it."

I just stood there watching as "Beau" drove away. I digested what just happened. So much for stereotypes. I closed the hood. I could not help thinking I am not in New York anymore. I got back in my car, started the ignition, and found my way to my temporary housing. I unloaded the car, settled in, and tried to get a good night's sleep. I could not. I was wound up from the three-day drive and pondered what it would be like to work at Maybelline. I still tried to reassure myself that I was doing the right thing. I was not yet in a place to dwell in the comfort of the cross.

It was now Monday morning, and I made my way to Maybelline. I could not help noticing that there was no traffic. I was so used to bumper to bumper traffic in New York. This was a pleasant shock to the system. I even commented on it when I arrived at the office. People looked at me like I was crazy. Everyone else agreed that traffic that morning was terrible. I was doing at least fifty-five miles per hour on the highway. In my mind, that was not traffic. Bumper to bumper is traffic. Another positive check mark on moving to Memphis. I entered the building and made my way to Human Resources. There is always that first-day paperwork that needs to be filled out. Another surprise. They were expecting me to show up on Tuesday, not Monday. Did I not understand the correct day and time through the southern drawl? We looked at each other, then just laughed it off. We worked it out.

After filling out all the paperwork, I was escorted to my new office and took a deep breath. I had to fight my nerves. I was introduced to my secretary. She gave me a big smile and I could not help but notice she was missing her front tooth. I could hear my mother telling me it is not polite to stare. I was rude. I could not help staring. The thought flashed before me, "how did you get this job? This is a cosmetics company!" In that moment, I stereotyped her and the south. In that moment, I started to see something I did not like. I was doing to them what had been done to me. I was being judgmental. I had allowed the hardness of New York and the façade of the beauty industry to infiltrate my soul. How could I be so blind? I realized I did have a strong opinion about the south and it was not good. I downplayed my initial reaction to "Beau" the day before. Apparently, I did not realize that Beau had opened my eyes that I was judgmental. I have always been one to take a hard look at myself. Sometimes I look for things that were not even there. Now I saw myself as judgmental. This was painful. With all my bumps and bruises, I saw myself as open-minded. Was I blind to my true self? Was I seeing some ugly? I groaned with the thought if this is only my second day in Memphis, what is next. I needed to shake that off and focus. I smiled back. I was, then, greeted by my new Associate Marketing Manager and my boss. I was now the Senior Marketing Manager on the Eye Business for Maybelline. Every woman knows Great Lash Mascara: and now, I was the keeper of the brand and felt the weight of the responsibility.

Even with the warm greeting, I knew they were sizing me up and I was doing the same with them. I wanted to make a good first impression. I wanted them to like me. I needed to fit in. I had been through so much. I just wanted to be me even though I was not sure who I was. I did not want to play a part to fit in. This was important to me. I was finally in a place where I asserted my independence and took the risk to move out of New York and away from my family. I needed a fresh start. Yet, the past would not let go. I still struggled to understand who I was. I struggled to accept me for me. I came from a different culture. I had a different mindset. I looked at life differently. I did not see that it was good that I brought a different perspective to things. I could not see that I brought a rainbow of color and I lit up a room. I did not see it because of years of hiding from others and myself. As a child, I hid in closets and under beds. As an adult, I hid from myself. I was suffocating and did not know it. I battled to come out from under the wall I built for myself. The wall I built for myself was red. It was red with anger, frustration, and disappointment. It was red with molten lava building up to an explosion from spending a lifetime trying to be what everyone else wanted me to be. I realized that in wanting to be accepted, I had become them.

One thing was clear. I was a New Yorker in Memphis So, right out of the gate, there was a clash of cultures. It was obvious that I was the everything is due yesterday type, and they were fixin' to do it. It baffled me. I did not know if they were going to do the job or not. I did not exactly endear myself to their hearts by asking, "Are you going to do it or just fixing to do it?" I spoke fast with a New York accent. I could not understand why they did not understand me. I knew I did not understand them. They spoke slow with a heavy southern drawl. I would often motion with my hands to speed it up. Fast paced was all I knew. It did not take long to realize that I did not fit in. Even something as simple as walking down the hall was a dead giveaway. I did not walk. I walked at running clip. It took a colleague to say, "I can always tell when you are coming down the hall. You're the only one who runs." That was an eyeopener. It hit me where I lived. I wanted a change, but I still wore my old shoes. I chose this change in my life. I should be able to adapt. I should be able to let go of deeply held beliefs. I should be able to let go of the shackles of the past and embrace my fresh start. I should be excited. Instead, I am scared. I do not know why.

As I was feeling my way through, I was confronted with the fact that my associate was doing everything before I arrived, and she was used to having people and management approach her for answers. Now I arrived, and I needed to establish myself as the new Senior Manager on the business. She was not happy, and she felt like she was being pushed aside. Instead of coming to me, she went to my boss who subsequently had a chat with me. My immediate reaction was a knot in the pit of my stomach. Was I failing already? Instead, I surprised myself. I decided to ignore that feeling of failure that was gripping me. It was a fight. It was more important to me not to fall into old habits of withdrawing from an uncomfortable situation. I needed to deal with this. From personal experience, I knew what it felt like to be pushed aside. I wanted to reassure her that we were a team. I set up a meeting with her and we had an open and honest conversation. I wanted to make sure she was responsible for her own projects and would be the point person. We would have status meetings to confirm everything was on track. I knew what it was like not to get direction. That is what I was there for. Our meeting was civil and productive. Problem solved. After that, we worked well together and were a good team. The longer we worked together, I became aware of something that was outside of my comfort zone. I trusted her and she trusted me. It was as if a ray of sunlight shone through a crack in my wall. I allowed myself to feel it.

I was grateful the problem with my associate was resolved quickly. But I had to simultaneously, deal with another problem. When I was fired from Chesebrough-Pond's, I was told I was not aggressive enough. Apparently, non-aggressive behavior in New York is aggressive behavior in Memphis. Our ad agency was in New York, and I flew back to New York with the marketing team for a major meeting. One evening, we all went out to dinner. It felt good to be on my home turf. I thought dinner conversation was lively, and we were all exchanged stories. I was getting to know my colleagues from Maybelline and my ad agency team. It was time to say good night. It was pouring rain outside, and we needed to get cabs to get back to the hotel. Hailing a cab in New York City is challenging enough, but in the rain, it is basically impossible. Enter the New Yorker. This is my town, and I stepped up to the challenge. Within minutes, I successfully hailed taxis. YES! Actually, NO! When we returned to Memphis, my boss called me into his office. I thought, "This cannot be good." Our Executive Vice President was very southern and very much a product of the gentile south. She considered the behavior I demonstrated in New York too aggressive, and it needed to be tempered. Excuse me? I did not understand why I was being singled out. We were getting to know each other. We told stories, laughed and we seemed to be enjoying the evening. As quiet as I can be, I am different when I tell stories. I am animated and flamboyant. The little actress would come out. Yet, it felt like every time I allowed my animated personality to come through, I would get shut down. I listened to what my boss had to say, and I did what I usually did. I started to withdraw. But again, something wonderful happened. I learned valuable lessons from my past, and I allowed myself to adjust to my new world. I did not fight it. Within three months, my "too aggressive" New York persona transformed into pleasantly assertive. It seems funny now, but pleasantly assertive is very much who I am. I believe in being respectful of others and working with people not running rough shod over them. The real me started to emerge. Was it possible that I would not have to play a role anymore to try and fit in?

I had some successes, but it seemed that my honeymoon period was filled with tests. Thankfully, I came through the aggression thing, but I was tested on several levels. One thing I learned over the years was that, even though I thought I was right, I needed to be wise in proving my point to management. I learned quickly that my ad agency worked from the top down. They presented advertising campaigns to management first and then the campaign decision would trickle down to the troops. My associate manager and I did not have a say. To be honest, this did not make me happy. We had been working with the agency to develop an advertising campaign for a new product being added to the Great Lash Mascara line. Management was in New York. My associate manager and I were in Memphis. Thankfully, my boss did what he could to include us in the process. He faxed three campaigns to us to review. As we looked them over, we just looked at each other. The two of us were not thrilled with the campaigns. There was one specific campaign that we hated. We felt it was offensive. When my boss called, he gleefully told me that a decision had been made, and lo and behold, they chose the campaign we hated. What to do? Experience taught me it is not a good idea to say I think you are wrong. Instead of saying that we disagreed, I said that we had some concerns and would like to discuss them when he returned to Memphis. He agreed. Before they returned to the office, the two of us had a meeting with Market Research. We developed a plan to test the campaign without breaking the bank. When my boss returned, we were ready with the plan and the necessary details. My associate, Market Research and I met with my boss and the Executive Vice President. I explained our concerns and how to quell them. The cost of the test was only $10,000. I said,

"This is Great Lash. $10,000 is small potatoes to ensure that we do not negatively impact the brand. They agreed.

Now the fun part. I needed to break the news to the agency. My account supervisor and account executive were in Memphis for our weekly meeting. I broke the news. It was not received well. They balked at doing the test. I could not believe my ears when my account executive said, "This campaign is approved. We cannot risk getting negative test results." Excuse me!?! I stood firm. I said, "I have explained our concerns. I would rather spend $10,000 to confirm that this campaign works instead of spending $500,000 in production costs and $5,000,000 in advertising to find out it does not. If the results are negative, we can adjust the campaign." They left in a huff. Within hours, the president of the ad agency called the Executive Vice President to strongly protest doing this test. Since my EVP was already on board, she insisted the test be done. In that moment, shades of the past started to fade. My management supported me instead of tearing me down.

I needed my management support, as doing this test was a painful process. The agency did everything possible to stall and disrupt the test from moving forward. We proceeded on two fronts. The test was initiated, and we kept moving forward to get the commercial ready for production. A month had passed, and I flew out to Los Angeles for the production meeting. We were scheduled to shoot the commercial in a few days. I arrived at my hotel and the results of the market research test results were faxed to the hotel and waiting for me upon arrival. I did not have time to look at them as I needed to get to the production meeting. While I was in the town car, I opened the envelope. I was overjoyed. The results vindicated me and my associate. Without getting too technical, if a commercial receives a 5% offensive rating, that was considered highly offensive. Our commercial scored 20% on the offensive rating scale. When I arrived at the production meeting, the president of the agency and her entire team were on a conference call with my management in Memphis. It was a heated discussion. To my surprise, my gentile, southern Executive Vice President was "aggressively" demanding that the commercial be changed. Oh, the irony. All I had to do was sit back and let my management fight it out with the agency. Finally, the agency agreed to the changes that needed to me made. The commercial was shot based on those changes. The results were amazing. We launched a new product into the Great Lash product line, and it did not take any sales away from the flagship brand. Unheard of. Soon after that, my boss came into my office, closed the door, and said he wanted to talk with me. Again, that gripping feeling. I looked at him. He sat down. He told me they were so grateful for the way I handled saving the brand from a possible negative impact, and they wanted to reward my efforts. He took an envelope out of his jacket pocket and handed me a surprise bonus. Sweet redemption. I finally learned how to effectively share my point of view without alienating management, compromising my deeply held ethics of letting my work speak for itself or compromising my integrity. Maybe I was not a failure after all. Once again, I chipped away at my wall.

I continued to feel my oats, but my old New York habits die hard. With everything going on in the first month, I was also called out about working late every night. I would stay late to get the job done. There was one big difference working in Memphis vs. working in New York. I needed to sign in in the morning and out at night. My boss noticed that I worked late. He came to my office, knocked on the door and closed it behind him. I was surprised that when he closed the door, I did not have a knot in my stomach. Was fear of authority starting to lift or was I starting to realize I did not need to keep waiting for the other shoe to drop. He sat down and said, "I notice your working late every night." I gave my typical New York response, "There's a lot of work to do." He looked at me and said, "This is not New York. We believe in a balanced life here. I want you out of here by 6:00 each night." Very rarely am I left speechless. I just looked at him. All I could manufacture was a nod of yes. I pondered. A balanced life. I did not even know what that meant. As he got up to leave, he turned and said, "By the way, you are doing a great job." I wanted to cry. I could not help thinking, "You mean I'm not a failure?"

Chapter 5
One Step at a Time

As directed, I would leave by 6:00 and head home. When I was home, I felt like a caged animal. I did not know what to do with myself. Staying late at the office was part of my DNA. Even though I went home, for what to me was early, I could not leave the office behind. I took work home with me. It seemed like a good alternative. It bothered me. The words balanced life kept resonating within me. A balanced life. I wondered what that felt like. It was now time to find out. As I paced, I thought about going out to eat. I never had time to cook, so I would usually pick up some food on the way home. I never thought about sitting at a table like a civilized human being. I discovered a Japanese restaurant on my way home. A Japanese restaurant in Memphis did not fit my preconceived notion. When I thought of restaurants in Memphis, I thought of fried chicken and barbecue. That fare was there, but Japanese? I, once again, came face to face with my stereotypical mindset. Later on, I even discovered an authentic Italian restaurant where the owners were from Brooklyn, NY. I was pleasantly surprised that getting out of the office enabled me to discover a whole new world. I decided to give the Japanese restaurant a try. Since I was alone, I would sit at the sushi bar. The restaurant had such ambiance and a peaceful quality about it. I noticed that the restaurant was adjacent to one of the major hospitals in the city. I noticed doctors entered the restaurant. I thought this must be good. And it was. At the sushi bar, the doctors and I would start to chat. That is how I found my doctors in Memphis. During our chats, I would find out about them and their backgrounds. I would ask about their education, their specialty and how long they were in practice. This was key in my finding my gynecologist. Since I had dealt with so many female problems, I wanted someone who would be sensitive to my health issues. One night, I chatted with a female doctor. She was a gynecologist. I found her to be so engaging, and she listened to what I was saying. I chose her to be my doctor. I was so pleased that I did. I even referred her to friends. Choosing a doctor this way gave me such a sense of security. This balanced life thing started to pay off.

Although Memphis was not New York, I managed to discover the cultural things I enjoyed. I got season tickets to the Orpheum Theater in downtown Memphis. It was one of the grand theaters of the south. I was stunned that parking was only $2.00 for the night. I was used to spending over $40.00 for parking in New York. I also enjoyed going to juried art shows. I loved poking around and talking to artists. I am always fascinated with how they are inspired to create their artwork. I discovered Memphis had two large, juried art shows per year. I loved it. To this day, I have an original piece of artwork hanging in my home that I purchased in Memphis. It is the first thing I see when I open my front door. I also went to the movies, and I found a Fred Astaire Dance Studio nearby. I was in heaven. I had no intention of competing, but taking lessons again transported me into my happy place. I started meeting people, and we would go out and dance the night away. Memphis was becoming my home.

As I carved out a life for myself, my faith was a major part of the balanced life. I discovered that the people at work were much more open talking about faith and going to church. My secretary new right away I was a Christian. Within my first month at work, I was hit with a strange circumstance. My secretary came into my office and asked if she could talk with me. She said it was personal. I asked her to close the door. She started crying. She blurted out that she was in a sinful relationship with a man who treated her badly. She knew she needed to get out of the relationship and get back with God. All I saw was her and not her missing tooth. I asked if I could pray with her. She quickly said yes. I do not remember what I prayed but it was along the lines of the Lord giving her the courage to lead the life that God wanted her to and to free her from this relationship. The following week, she got a call at work. She was hysterical. Her boyfriend had a massive heart attack and died. I just hugged her. I said, "I hope you'll see him in heaven." Through her tears, she quickly responded, "No, she wouldn't. He was a really bad man." After that I got the reputation of someone who prayed powerful prayers.

Showing my support, I went to the funeral. I had never been to a black funeral before. Being Italian, I was used to having the wake first. Of course, everyone was dressed in head to toe black and there was weeping. There was also a din of noise from conversation and laughter. I was often struck how people used the wake as an opportunity to catch up with family and friends they had not seen for a while. Then the funeral and the big food fest afterward. This time, I was taken aback by the heavy wailing by so many attendees. I was uncomfortable. I wanted to recede into the background, but my whiteness stood out in the crowd. I learned that there were white churches and black churches. Segregation was alive and well, even in God's house. That did not sit well with me. It fit right into my stereotypical narrative of the south. I had to get passed it. My secretary was so comforted that I was there for her. My prayers for her and attending the funeral brought us closer together. My humanness overrode my wall of protection. She trusted me, and it was obvious she had my back. She rededicated her life to the Lord, and we talked openly about spiritual things. I was grateful.

One thing became clear early on was that I needed to find a church. I remembered being told find an Assembly of God Church. So, I did. It was strange. I was a new believer and did not understand many things. I just knew, when I attended one church, I had the feeling "this church is dead." I found another church which was close to where I lived. They met at the agricenter which was five minutes away. I would cut through it to get to and from work. I soon learned what the agricenter was. Animals. Lots of animals. When I first started to cut through the agricenter, I made a wrong turn and came face to face with bison. I am a city girl. Bison! Even though they were behind a fence, I felt panic. These animals were huge. Besides the size of the bison, one thing was very noticeable. There was a pungent odor of manure. I did not know what was worse. The smell of urine in an enclosed subway or the heavy smell of livestock and their droppings wafting in the air. This sealed the deal that I was not in New York City anymore.

I adapted to the smell of livestock, as I started to call this Assembly of God Church my church home. As a new believer, I moved from being Catholic to non-denominational evangelical congregational to diving headfirst into a charismatic Spirit filled church. Again, it was God where do you have me now? I learned about supernatural healing.

I learned about praying in tongues. I discovered Christian television 24/7. I personally learned that God was the God of miracles. During my first month in Memphis, I was overcome with God letting me know He was with me. When I went to Memphis, I was $10,000 in debt. I had medical bills that I could not pay. When I left, I worked out a plan with the doctors to pay them a certain amount each month until the debt was paid off. I think they doubted that the debt would be paid. Thankfully, I had a New York salary on a Memphis cost of living. It felt so good to deposit my first paycheck. Since I tend to be meticulous about my finances, I checked my first month's bank statement. I noticed there was more money in my account than there should have been. I contacted the bank and said, "There must be a mistake." They checked my account and said it was accurate. I did not understand how I could make such a mistake. I account for every penny. It happened the second month. Again, accurate. Then it hit me. The Lord miraculously put money in my bank account. At first, I think I was in shock. This kind of thing does not happen. But it did. The only explanation was that it was a miracle. I was out of debt in only 10 months. Even on my New York salary, that would not have been possible. I now had experienced a tangible expression of God. He knew my financial need, and He showed up. From childhood, I believed that God was out there somewhere. God was shifting that paradigm. He was teaching me that He was close. He was teaching me that He was personal. He moved from using clouds in the shape of a cross to encourage me to using a financial miracle to show me He was with me. Before I asked Jesus into my heart, I knew about Him. Now I was hungry to know Him. In my hunger to know Him, I got involved in the church.

I went to prayer meetings. I learned about intercession and the gifts of the Holy Spirit. In doing so, I discovered that I moved in the spiritual gift of prophecy. When I was unemployed and devouring the scriptures, one of the first scriptures I read was 1 Corinthians 14:1 (NKJV) "Pursue love, and desire spiritual gifts, but especially that you may prophesy." Since God was the ultimate authority and this was His word, I said Okay, I desire the higher gift. I desire that I may prophesy. I did not register the pursue love part, just the prophesy part. I was now able to identify why I usually knew things before they happened. One specific event was the time my sister went on a ski weekend with a friend and her fiancé. They did not tell my sister that one of his friends would be there. It was basically a set up. My sister came home and told me, "I think I've met someone." I asked her to tell me about it. Without hesitating, I announced, "He's going to call you on Tuesday to ask you to get together for a drink on Thursday which will turn into dinner. You'll be engaged by September and married by May." That is exactly what happened.

I was not being trained up in the prophetic gift, I was just told I had it. The ladies room became my revelation room. Oftentimes, I would be in the church service, and I would feel a stirring deep inside. I would leave the service and go the ladies room. On one Sunday morning, I was in the ladies room and the pastor's wife came in. She saw me sitting on the sofa and I seemed very agitated. She asked me what was going on. I said I did not know. I feel this urgency bubbling up inside of me. I feel like I am going to say something, but I do not know what it is. That is when she formally announced to me that it was the gift of prophecy. Okay. Now what? I basically moved into the school of the Holy Spirit. I was often chastened for not following protocol. I did not know there was protocol. I would often be so overcome with the presence of God I would fall to the ground. I did not understand why that would happen. Again, I was ridiculed and chastened. The pastor said to me, "It's just not possible for someone to be slain in the spirit that much. Stop it." With such a stern admonishment, I felt I was being punished. I certainly could not talk to him about what was happening to me. My only option was to be obedient. I started to quench the Holy Spirit. It was painful. I felt saddened for two specific reasons. I quenched the Holy Spirit and the gift within me. And, once again, I felt that I did not fit in. I did not understand why God would allow these spiritual things to happen to me and then let me get ridiculed for it.

One weekend, I flew to Connecticut to visit my sister and her family. I sensed I was to attend the church that a dear friend attended. I showed up and she was so happy to see me. I sat with her and her husband. As we worshipped, I felt that urgent stirring deep within me. I thought I was going to explode. I was on my knees weeping. Suddenly, there was a lull in the worship. I exploded. I started to prophesy. Words poured out of me. I could not quench it. It was as if the Holy Spirit took over, and I had no say in the matter. From what I remember, I said,

"There's pride here." That is all I remember. That did not go over well. The choir cranked up louder. Then, the pastor jumped off the platform, came toward me waving his finger and accusing me of disrupting the service and sternly said, "that was not from God." My normal reaction would have been to crumble under the weight of being openly criticized in front of a church. The most amazing thing happened. I sat there quietly praying in my prayer language. I felt this wall of protection form around me; and I saw his words hit the wall and just melt to the floor. Things erupted after that and there was a major discussion in the service. My friend's husband said they had prayed for a prophet to speak into the house, and this is the way you treat her." Me? What does that mean? I am not even sure what I am doing, and now he is giving me a title. Shades of the past emerged. In that moment, I wanted to run. I wanted to hide. I wanted to scream. I was just being obedient. I felt rejected. I felt angry. I felt confused. I wondered why God would let this happen. When the service finished, my friend, her husband and I were in the parking lot chatting. I was unnerved but peaceful at the same time. They assured me I did the right thing. I explained I could not seem to control the words coming out of me. It just happened. They each gave me a big hug. As I left them and returned to Memphis, I prayed about what happened in church that day. I asked the Lord to help me understand. He did. He showed me I was on an assignment. A prophet.

A week after I returned to Memphis my friend called me. She said she needed to share what transpired at the church that led up to Sunday's events. She told me that a born-again Jew was an elder in the church. He met with the church leadership and told them that there was pride there. They responded by kicking him out of the church. I was stunned as I tried to process what she was telling me. Then she quoted the scripture verse Luke 8:17 (NKJV), "For nothing is secret that will not be revealed, nor anything hidden that will not be known and come to light." Her words encouraged me as she confirmed that the Lord had used me. But I was conflicted. I knew it was scriptural. I was hungry for more of God. The Lord had shown me that He is real. Jesus is real. The Holy Spirit is real. But, instead of focusing on the reality of them and the experiences, I let my humanness take over. I focused on how I was feeling instead of what I knew to be true. I put myself on a diet. I felt hurt. I felt rejected. I was operating in a world I did not fully understand. Even though I felt God's protection in the church, I felt I needed to protect myself. God let this happen. How can I trust Him? I know I can trust myself.

Time went on. I started teaching a Sunday bible study for adult singles. I was asked by leadership to consider it. I prayed about teaching and felt I got the green light to do so. My tendency to overstudy and overprepare operated in full throttle. I did not want to get anything wrong. I did not want to be reprimanded or punished. The pastor had already chastened me for succumbing to the Holy Spirit. I did not want to be criticized for something else. I wanted to break free from the stranglehold of authority, but it was so entrenched in me since my days as a child in Catholic School. I was taught to speak when I was spoken to. I was taught to do what I was told and not question authority. Now I was agitated, and I started to question authority. I felt like a caterpillar that was stuck in a cocoon. I wanted to break out and be a butterfly. I was trying to figure out how. Despite my humanness, I knew if I prayed about each lesson the Lord would show up. He did. I felt ready for each lesson. I did enjoy studying and preparing for each class. I was frustrated though. The church had a group of about forty adult singles. Maybe two or three would show up for bible study on Sunday morning before the service, but the whole group would show up for social gatherings. Somehow, I got roped into planning and organizing these get togethers. I did not want to do it. I did not have the time to do it. I did not have the patience to do it. I did not have the love to do it.

My hunger for the Word continued to grow. I was not satisfied. One day I chatted with my secretary about it. She mentioned that on Tuesday evenings one of the elders at her church taught a bible study. She was currently teaching on the book of Psalms. This intrigued me, and I decided to attend. It took me an hour to travel to the church after a full day's work. I was welcomed. I must confess, I was a bit uncomfortable. This was a black church in the south. I stood out. I was more bothered by my whiteness than they were. Before the study began each week, there was a time of prayer. They focused on praying not on me. I focused on them. I noticed they paced when they prayed. I still prayed on my knees. My plan was to sit there and not actively participate. They prayed loudly. My plan was to sit there quietly. I was way outside my comfort zone. At first, I tried to stick to my plan. I sat there and prayed quietly. I felt I did not want to pray wrong and be called out for it. Without realizing it, the fear of being punished pushed me back into an old habit. In trying to conform, I climbed into the church box. I needed to do what was acceptable. I needed to fit in. God changed all of that. He did not just open the box. He ripped it open and pulled me out. One evening, as I was sitting in the prayer meeting, I felt that all too familiar stirring deep within me. The teacher saw that something was happening. She came over to me. Suddenly, she put her hand on my stomach and said, "Let it out! Let it out!" Prayers started bubbling out of me with such intensity. Then, prophetic words started bubbling up as well. I fought it. I was sobbing. I wanted to quench the Holy Spirit. That is what I knew to do. Now I was being given the freedom to let the Holy Spirit move. Prayers exploded. Prophetic words exploded. When things calmed down, the teacher and the other elders reinforced that night that I had a strong prophetic anointing. But, again, that was it.

I attended the Assembly of God Church for two years. I felt that things were shifting at the church. I sensed that I was to leave. I was not sure why and I prayed about it. When I joined the church, the focus was on the things of God. The church was now in the early stages of building its own church facility. The focus became fundraising and bringing in money. This did not sit well with me. One Sunday evening, I was in service. The Holy Spirit was moving. By this point, I had many personal experiences, and recognized that the Lord was making Himself known. I recognized the presence of God when I worshipped the Lord. I would get lost in worship with tears streaming down my face. On this Sunday evening, I was lost in worship. Suddenly, the pastor stopped the worship and started to announce a new fundraising campaign. I was so angry. I did not know if this was righteous anger or me, but I left the service. I beat myself up for leaving the service, but the anger would not go. As I tried to understand what I was feeling, it hit me. At first, the pastor quenched the Holy Spirit in me. Now he quenched the Holy Spirit for everyone. He was more focused on money and building a church building instead of housing the Holy Spirit and allowing Him free reign. I felt this grieved the Holy Spirit. It grieved me. It became clear that this was no longer the place for me. It was time to start breaking free of my cocoon. It was time to listen to the Holy Spirit within me and not be intimated by authority. It was time to leave.

I felt a pulling to attend the church where I was taking bible study on Tuesday evenings. It was a little strange. Being the only white person in a bible study on Tuesday evenings was one thing. But this was church on Sunday. There was only one other white person who attended. As I have said, I did not like to stand out. My intention was to sit at the back of the church. The bible study teacher was an elder, and she insisted I sit in the front row. I was not happy. She physically grabbed my hand and brought be forward. To say I was uncomfortable is an understatement. After attending for a few weeks, I started to get that intensity deep within. I did not know what to do. So, I got up and went to the back of the church. I could not stay still. I paced back and forth, back, and forth. I felt that I was a distraction, so I went to, where else, the ladies room. I remember I wound up on my knees in the lady's room. Prophetic words poured out of me. I did not realize that someone had come in, saw what was happening and went out to get the teacher. From what I was told, she entered the lady's room and was knocked to the floor by the power of the Holy Spirit. In the sea of Holy Spirit fog, I heard her say, "This word needs to be given in the sanctuary." She left and brought back two burly ushers. They lifted me off the floor, held me up and brought me back into the sanctuary. I could not stand on my own. Somewhere in all of this, I lost my shoes. The teacher got up on the platform and stopped the service. She explained that the Lord had a word to give through me. The ushers brought me to the microphone. The intensity started again, and the prophetic words poured out. Only, this was different. The Holy Spirit called out sin after sin in the church. I have no idea how long this lasted. This time no one chastened me in front of the whole church. This time I was allowed to speak. Once finished, I was carried to the front row. The service started up again. I was still under the anointing of the Holy Spirit and was out for the count for quite a while. As I look back and remember that day, two major things stood out to me. First, as the service concluded I was now fully aware of what was happening. Instead of the usual milling about at the end of a service, things got quiet. Suddenly, without invitation, people started going to the altar and confessing their sins. I sat there overwhelmed and in awe at the same time. Part of me thought no one would notice if I slipped out of the church quietly.

The other part of me wanted to sit there and pray for all the people submitting to God and confessing their sins. Sitting there and praying won out. Second, when the ushers placed me in a seat, the coat dress I was wearing opened and exposed the lower part of my legs. My secretary was in the choir loft. She saw what was happening, came out of the choir loft, took off her choir robe and placed it over my lap. I do remember opening my eyes and seeing her black hand on my white hand and thinking, "this is the way it's supposed to be."

I managed to get myself home. The following Tuesday evening, I planned to attend the prayer meeting and the bible study. Unfortunately, I was running late from work. I arrived after the prayer time. As I approached the entrance to the classroom, I heard a discussion in progress. I did not want to interrupt, so I waited outside the door. What I heard disturbed me. The discussion was about me and what happened on Sunday morning. One woman said, "Who does that white woman think she is?" She sounded so angry. Was she angry because I was white? Was she angry because I called out sins in the church? Or was she angry because I was white and used by God? The teacher responded by saying, "She was under the anointing, and the Holy Spirit was speaking through her." I started shaking. All I heard was who does that white woman think that she is? I needed to get out of there as fast as I could. I could not possibly go to class. I raced to my car. I started crying out to the Lord. "I do not understand. You seem to be moving through me. I keep getting slammed. I do not seem to fit in anywhere. Help me. Show me what to do." The next day I went to work, and my secretary came into my office. She asked me why I did not come to class the night before. I told her what happened. She hugged me. I never went back.

Once again, my humanness took over. I needed to self-protect. I did not pray about leaving. I went with my feelings. My departure was so abrupt that I did not know where to go next. After praying, I sensed I was to go back to the first Assembly of God Church I attended when I arrived in Memphis. When I returned, I realized something had changed. The church I once thought was dead was alive. And it was racially mixed. Thank you, Jesus. I started to settle in and made some friends. Then, during worship, that all too familiar intensity would show up. When it did, I could not contain it. Prophetic words bubbled out of me. I did not notice any protocol in giving prophetic words. The words I delivered became stronger, and they had disciplinary tone to them. No one in leadership ever said anything to me, but all I kept hearing was who does that white woman think that she is. I felt compelled to make an appointment with the pastor. I needed guidance. What I got I did not expect. He was cordial and we said our opening pleasantries. I then started to explain the purpose of meeting with him. I asked for his guidance about the prophetic words that would come through me and how strong they seemed. I needed to know what he thought. I needed to know what to do when it happened. He just looked at me and said, "Do you want to give these words?" I nervously said, "No, I don't." He then said, "Then, I know it is God. I'm not sure how to lead you in this." I thanked him and said goodbye. I felt alone.

Chapter 6
Help Me

Even though I felt alone after talking to my pastor, I was not. I was building a life for myself. I was so happy, especially during the first two years. I was discovering me. I now embraced the south. I rediscovered things I love to do. I was making friends. On the work front, things were progressing nicely. I made fast friends with the Manager of Market Research. We were both from New York and lived close to each other. I so missed going to Broadway shows that we decided to get season tickets to the Orpheum Theater downtown. The first time we arrived for a selected show, we realized very quickly we were not in New York anymore. We mirrored the way we would dress to attend the theater on Broadway. We were nicely dressed but casual by Memphis standards. Everyone else was dressed to the nines – gowns, furs, formal suits for the men. My friend and I just looked at each other. We chuckled at the fact that we stood out like sore thumbs. I remember the time I went to see Joseph and the Amazing Technicolor Dream Coat. I sat in the fourth row of the orchestra. I did not know what to expect from the show, but I found it so creative and funny. There was a scene where pharaoh was Elvis. When he said, "I just love being the king," I roared with laughter. It felt so good to laugh again. It just burst forth and reverberated through every part of me. My laugh reverberated throughout the Orpheum theater. People looked at me like I was crazy. I did not care. I enjoyed the show, and I remember it to this day.

I took a weekend trip with a friend from work to Nashville. She was from San Francisco so, we shared that cosmopolitan vibe and hit off. I thoroughly enjoyed Nashville. We just had to do the Nashville thing and visit the Grand Ole' Opry. It was fun to go through the park and experience such a landmark of country music history. As we made our way through Nashville, I was pleasantly surprised with juried art show right smack in the center of Nashville at one of the major parks. We meandered through the show, and I happened upon an artist. His work captivated me. We chatted, and I told him I was looking for pottery to put on my bedroom dresser. I loved his work, but what he had displayed was not quite working for me. He generously offered to design pottery for me. My creative side came through and I worked with him to design my custom-made pieces. The pottery sits on my dresser to this day. To cap off the day, we discovered an Italian restaurant called Mario's. It was probably one of the best Italian meals I have ever had. That is saying a lot coming from a first-generation Italian American from Brooklyn. I loved it so much, I recommended it to my parents when they visited me. My mother was the ultimate Italian cook. She raved about it. I recommended it to my brother-in-law a few years ago. Sadly, He told me it closed.

I also visited Tulsa with a friend of mine from church. I did not know what to expect. A colleague from work was from Tulsa, and he recommended great restaurants and things to do. My friend and I had different interests. We accommodated each other. I am enthralled with museums. The Phillbrook Museum of Art did not disappoint. My friend was not a museum lover. She was gracious and tolerated my need to visit every exhibit. I am embarrassed to say I do not remember what we did to suit her taste. We found restaurants that suited both our tastes. She was more into spicy food, and I was more into American and Italian. I remember she ordered a spicy shrimp dish appropriately named firecracker shrimp. I could feel the heat coming from her plate. She took one bite, and her mouth was on fire. Tears flowed from her eyes. She could not speak. I looked at her like she was crazy for ordering such spicy food. I asked her, "Are you okay?" Through the fire, she nodded her head yes and smiled. I could not understand how eating food that burns your mouth so badly could possibly be enjoyable. My sensitive stomach balked at the thought.

The Lord took care of that. One night I went out to eat at Brooklyn Bridge. I had to be careful what I ordered as too many foods made me sick. As I parked my car, I had this overwhelming desire for a salad. I could not eat salad. Everything I ate had to be cooked and plain. I tried to ignore that strong desire. I did not want to be sick. As I sat down at a table and looked at the menu, that desire for a salad was so strong. It would not go away. Was the Holy Spirit trying to tell me something? The Lord miraculously put money in my bank account. Did He heal me of IBS? I took a step of faith. I ordered a salad. I was nervous about eating it. It was so hard to break out of the fear of food making me sick. I lived in that fear for so long. The waiter served my salad. It was beautiful. It was full of color with fresh vegetables and a mix of salad greens. I just looked at it. It was raw. I prayed. I gulped. I took my fork and gently took some salad. I looked at my fork. I took a deep breath and took a bite. I closed my eyes as the flavors burst in my mouth. I took another bite and another. It was so delicious. I headed home. After four hours, I realized I did not get sick from the salad. I was fine. I was beyond overjoyed. I paid attention to what I was sensing. I have been enjoying salad ever since.

Overall, life was good, except I was getting a lot of colds and sinus infections. I later discovered that Memphis had one of the worst air qualities in the country. This little detail was never mentioned to me during the interviewing process. My nose was always stuffed up. I lacked sleep, and I found myself living at the doctor's office. The doctor prescribed medications to counteract my cold and sinus symptoms. They did not help. I was finally referred to an allergist. Even though I knew I had hay fever, I had never been to an allergist before. I was told that the tests would take about four hours. They took an hour and a half. The doctor said I was the most allergic person he had ever met. I even had an allergic reaction to allergy shot that was supposed to help me. My arm swelled up and was very red. It was painful. The doctor prescribed several medications. I was so desperate to feel better that I did not even ask about the medications being prescribed. That would come back to haunt me. Even though I took the mediations for four years. I did not feel better. It never occurred to me to question the doctor. He knew more than me. I did not listen to my body. I did not use my common sense. I just lived with it. I had overcome so much, this seemed minor in comparison.

I was happy that I found my footing at Maybelline and enjoyed my work and the people who worked with me. The one exception was my boss. He was a nice man and knowledgeable. Only, he needed to work on his people skills. He micromanaged not only me but everyone else. I had no problem reporting to someone; but I needed to be free to do my job. My management style was more on a macro level. I trusted my staff to do their jobs and then some. I had oversight, and things worked well. He used to do this power thing with me. I would have a meeting scheduled with him, and I would arrive on time. Knowing I was there, he would keep his back to me and continue doing whatever he was doing. He kept me waiting sometimes ten minutes before acknowledging my existence. At first, I sat there and waited patiently. Over time, my patience shifted to frustration. As an example, in one of my meetings with him, I reviewed the analytics on the business and made a recommendation on how to proceed on the issue at hand. He made me sit there, and he redid the analytics his way. Without fail, we came to the same conclusion even though I approached things from a different perspective. I felt like it was a big waste of time. I will never forget that in one meeting with him I realized he was about to reanalyze my analysis. I just looked at him and said, "I'm leaving. Call me when you're finished." Not even a blip. He did his thing. I did my thing. He called when he was finished. I went back to his office and oohla! Same conclusion.

I was not alone in my frustration. Many staff members and support teams complained about working with him. As management became aware of the issues people had with him, they decided to do what is called a 360-degree evaluation. Everyone who worked with him needed to provide evaluations. For some reason, I worked well with him. I was selected to meet with him weekly to assess him and the evaluations. This was not fun. We were both uncomfortable. I tried to deliver the assessments professionally and without bias. He tried to receive the information without appearing upset. He did not have a poker face.

One of the big issues was that he expected everyone to fit his mold.

I had first-hand experience. As I mentioned, I was so happy at Maybelline. They treated me well, and I felt I finally fit in. Or so I thought. Maybelline was active in the community and was a patron of the Memphis Opera. I loved opera and had season tickets to the New York City opera. One day, management wanted to introduce the arts to employees. There was to be a special performance by the Memphis

Opera in the cafeteria during the lunch hour. It is an interesting experience to listen to opera while pots, pans, and dishes clanked in the background. I had to tune the background noise out and focus on the music. I sat at one of the tables and was introduced to the Director of the Memphis Opera. I was intrigued that he was Chinese with a southern accent. It seemed like such a contradiction. After a moment, I was able to focus on our conversation. We chatted for a while. I told him how much I enjoyed opera and that I had season tickets to the New York City Opera. I told him my favorite aria was E Lucevan Le Stelle from Tosca. He looked at me and smiled. He excused himself. I did not think twice about it. The next thing I knew he was at the microphone and announced that he was changing the program. The next aria would E Lucevan Le Stelle from Tosca. He dedicated the aria to me. It took a moment to register what he said. I then reacted with a squeak of glee. I was in heaven. Everything and everyone seemed to disappear. I closed my eyes and became one with the music. I was moved. I laughed and cried at the same time. When the aria was finished, I wiped my eyes and gave an exhilarated standing ovation. I could feel people looking at me. I turned my head. My boss and some colleagues were laughing at me. I was so caught up; it did not bother me. Instead, I looked at them and joked, "Maybe you just need to be Italian to understand." I left it there. My boss did not.

Soon after that day, my boss came to my office and closed the door.

He abruptly said, "We need to talk." From the sound of his voice I asked, "Is there a problem?" He said, "You laugh too much." Not understanding, I said, "Excuse me? Again, you laugh too much. And that display during the aria in the cafeteria, well, it is unprofessional. You need to watch it."

He left my office. I just sat there in disbelief. How can being happy be a problem? I do admit that my laugh is very hearty and infectious. I guess my response to the aria was the tipping point for him. How could I not see the signs? I thought things were going so well. I felt comfortable. I felt like I discovered the real me. I fit in. I made progress. I worked well with management. I worked well with colleagues. The reality hit me that the problem was bigger than my laugh. The problem was I could not be myself. This problem seemed to follow me wherever I went. What was I not getting? I was conflicted. I was emerging from my cocoon as a butterfly. His words cut deep. I clipped my wings. I withdrew. My joy turned into sadness. My laughter was once again, silenced. After a few months, my boss showed up at my office door, came in, closed the door, and said, "We need to talk." I groaned. I looked at him and said, "Is there a problem? He said, "You don't laugh anymore." "Excuse me!?!" "You don't laugh anymore." I said, "you said I laugh too much. It's unprofessional." He said, "People are noticing you don't laugh anymore." I wanted to just scream at him. Instead, I said, "So, you want me to laugh again." "Yes." He then got up and left. I closed the door. I was angry. I thought, "You are giving me permission to laugh again. You are giving me permission to be myself. How dare you!" After that, I could not look at him. I did not want to be around him. I felt I was living under a microscope. The damage was done. I lost my balance. I did not know how to be myself.

My response was to do my job. I was rewarded. I was promoted to Director of Marketing on the relaunch of a major product line. The line originally launched in a decentralized approach with each category delegated to that specific team. For example, the eye products of the brand were under my direction. The face products were under the face team and so on. The brand needed to be under one umbrella. It was wonderful to be recognized and promoted, but the task at hand was daunting. Under the decentralized approach, eight people were managing the different products in the line. When the line became centralized under my direction, only my manager and myself would manage all categories in the line. We quickly needed to assess the status of each category and develop a complete brand strategy. My balanced life disappeared. I now worked long hours. My boss no longer insisted that I leave at 6:00. I traveled around the country and met with accounts. I laid out the relaunch of the brand. I did not feel at all well. I did not know what to do about my health. I thought about leaving Memphis. I discovered that several people left Maybelline because of the air quality and being sick. My boss in his inimitable way said, "You have to do what you have to do."

Things were even challenging with my ad agency. The strategy for the brand had been approved and key products would be advertised.

The agency was in Memphis for a meeting to present campaign ideas. As a marketing team, we had painstakingly laid out the creative objectives and the product benefits which were approved by management. When the campaigns were presented, I noticed that the product benefits that sell the product were missing from the advertising. I asked about it. The president of the agency told me that they determined they were not necessary. I challenged her. It quickly deteriorated into a screaming match. I said, "It is obvious all the work we did means nothing!" I was so angry. I stormed out of the meeting leaving them, my boss, and the Executive Vice President in my wake. As I stormed back to my office, shades of the past came flooding in. "I'm so getting fired over this." I got to my office and slammed the door. I paced trying to calm down. There was a knock at the door. I hesitated. I opened my office door. Standing there was the president of the agency. I just glared at her. The next moment stunned me. She put out her hand to shake mine. She said, "I want to thank you. I love working with someone who is so passionate about what they do and fights for it." We worked it out so all of us were happy with the final campaign. It was a home run. I had an epiphany. I had grown. I stood up for myself. I fought for what I believed in. I was assertive. I was unapologetic.

Tension continued to remain in the air. Rumors were flying that the company was about to be sold. I had been through this so many times before. I prayed that the rumors were not true. They were true. The company was sold to Cosmair, the parent company to L'Oreal and Lancome. I was not happy. If an offer to remain with Maybelline was extended to me, it meant I would be relocated back to New York. I was extended an offer, but I waited to accept it. I knew what working in New York was like. Been there. Done that. I wanted to explore other job opportunities. I was in a time crunch because I needed to give my answer by a certain date. I went on interviews, but no new job opportunities materialized. I accepted the offer and prepared myself physically and emotionally to move back to New York. I was given a very lucrative relocation package. I negotiated a better deal. Since I never bought a home in Memphis, I negotiated including my original deal with Maybelline which covered many home expenses not included in the Lancome package. They agreed. I started the arduous task of flying back and forth to New York to look for a place to live.

Business meetings also brought me to New York. The process of merging the two companies was in full throttle. In May 1996, I was in New York for a PR meeting. I was scheduled to fly back to Memphis that evening. The weather said otherwise. Heavy lightning and thunderstorms delayed or canceled many flights. Mine included. I was at LaGuardia Airport amidst the crush of people trying to reschedule flights. I turned to meet up with coworkers when I tripped over a man's luggage. I crashed to the ground. I was in shock and screamed in pain. I was taken to a hospital in Queens. They took x-rays which were inconclusive. I certainly could not fly to Memphis. I was in dire straits. My parents were on vacation, so I called my aunt and uncle who lived in Brooklyn. They came to the hospital and brought me back to the home I grew up in. The next day they made an appointment for me with an orthopedic doctor. He took additional x-rays and determined that I tore my meniscus. He put me in an immobilizer and said I could not fly for at least three weeks. I was nursed by my aunt and uncle at my childhood home.

My mobility was limited. I stayed in my parent's apartment which was on the upper level. Stairs were a challenge, so there I stayed for most of my time there. One day I made it downstairs to my aunt and uncle's apartment. I needed the visit. My grandmother, who was dealing with dementia, came into the apartment. She looked at me and paused. I did not know if she recognized me or not. She said, "How did you get so big?" That hurt more than the pain in my knee. Even with dementia, she had the wherewithal to cut me down and hit a deep nerve. My aunt just looked at me. It was at that moment that I was hit with the reality that something was seriously wrong. I did not know what it was.

After two weeks, my parents returned from vacation to find an unpleasant surprise. They were stunned to see me there immobile and in pain. They quickly rose to the challenge and took care of me. It had been a long time since I appreciated being mothered. After three weeks, I received the green light from the doctor to return to Memphis. I was still wearing the immobilizer and managed to navigate the airport. The flight home was difficult.

When I returned home, I immediately made an appointment with an orthopedic surgeon in Memphis. He thoroughly examined me and decided to take the conservative route to see how I would heal. My knee was so swollen, and the pain was excruciating. He gave me a cortisone shot. I now had to deal with transitioning to my new company and management, looking for a home in New York all while in pain. This felt like I was reliving my move to Connecticut all over again. I had to ask the question why, does this keep happening to me.

After several trips house hunting in New York, I found a townhome in Tarrytown, NY. I felt at home the minute I hobbled into the door. This time the depressed real estate market played in my favor. I called a dear friend in New York who was a realtor and a tough negotiator. He guided me through the whole process and suggested I put in a low-ball offer. I was concerned that they would just turn it down. He knew best. With a little bit of haggling. they accepted my offer. Since I was in Memphis, he oversaw all the inspections and the closing process. The deal was set, and the day was approaching to leave Memphis.

Unfortunately, there was a glitch. I was scheduled to relocate to New York in September 1996. My doctor determined that I was not healing properly and scheduled me for surgery the week before I was to relocate. I was supposed to have arthroscopic surgery. I had been through that before when I dislocated the same knee playing volleyball. I figured no biggie. I will be up and around in no time. I kept things moving for the relocation. I arranged for the moving company to move me out the week after my surgery. I crossed my I's and dotted my T's. Everything was in place.

The day of the surgery arrived. I was emotionally ready for it. I wanted to be awake and opted for a local anesthetic in my knee. The moment my doctor went into my knee to repair the meniscus he said, "Knock her out." That is the last thing I remember. I found out later that my meniscus was shredded. He had to cut deep into my knee to try and repair the damage. Even though the surgery did not go as planned, I went home thinking it would be okay to fly to New York in a few days. The movers came as scheduled. They took everything including my car. I was now ready to fly to New York. I spent the night at a Memphis airport hotel. In the middle of the night, I woke up screaming in pain. It felt like every nerve ending in my right leg was on fire. I called the doctor's emergency number. He advised that I get housekeeping to bring ice to my room. He also said I was to cancel my flight and come into the office the next day. I was beside myself. This cannot be happening. I am supposed to start my new life tomorrow. I could not sleep. The pain was excruciating.

I arrived for my doctor's appointment. I was in tears. He examined me. I was not prepared for his diagnosis. He said, "You have developed RSD – reflex sympathetic dystrophy. I said, "What does that mean?" He explained that after an injury, the body can react by taking on sympathetic nerve pain which is worse than the original injury. I asked him, "what do we do?" I could not register what he said next. He said, "We manage the pain. There is no cure."

I felt like I had been run over by a truck. No cure! What do you mean no cure? I am starting a new life. I cannot live like this. What am I supposed to do now? He just looked at me and said I could not fly for at least two weeks. He needed to get me on a pain management program. I was reeling. I contacted my boss and told him the bad news. I could not get to New York for at least two weeks. I had to assign my parents power of attorney to close on my home. I was now homeless.

Management decided to put me up at the Holiday Inn in Memphis as part of my relocation package. It was determined that all my needs would be met living at a hotel instead of temporary housing. I settled in at the Holiday Inn for the duration. It was a good plan, but I was informed by the hotel management that I could only stay for two weeks. They were completely booked after that. I prayed and prayed and prayed.

Two weeks dragged by and I, finally, had my follow-up visit with my doctor. He gave me the clearance to fly to New York. After what I had been through, I was nervous about traveling. It felt like the flight was more than two hours long. I arrived and a wheelchair was waiting for me. At that moment, I wished I had a special someone waiting for me. I felt like I was going through the motions. Go to baggage claim. Find my bags. Point them out. Find my parents. Drive to my new home. I was grateful that my parents were there for me, but I found it ironic that I left them and exerted my independence four years before, and now I was dependent on them again. The excitement I was supposed to feel was displaced by pain and fear. My parents stayed with me to make sure

I could manage well. I struggled because my new townhome had two levels. When I managed to get to the first floor, I stayed there for the day until I needed to go back upstairs to go to bed. I felt like my new home was a prison. I was trapped even though I had the key. Adapting to my new home, the next challenge was getting to work. My normal route was to take the metro north train to Grand Central station every day then back home. This was now impossible. Since I was injured on the job, management arranged to have a town car pick me up at home in the morning and then bring me back home at night. This went on for a couple of months, and it was expensive. Even with this precaution, I still had to put in full days at the office. I put a great deal of stress on my knee and the pain, once again, was excruciating. I called my doctor in Memphis. He referred me to a doctor in New York who pioneered knee replacement surgery. He examined me and then gave me the bad news. He said that I damaged my knee again and needed another surgery. I cannot even remember how I reacted to the news. It is all a blur.

I had the second surgery. The doctor discovered that I tore the meniscus again. This time the doctor removed about 50% of the meniscus. The major complication was that I was dealing with RSD. He put me on a physical therapy program with a therapist in the city. I needed to take time off from work to go to physical therapy. It was not helping. I was in so much pain. I could not bend my knee or do any of the required exercises. My leg was also numb. I discovered that the veins were not working properly. Blood flow to my leg was impaired. I needed to wear a rubberized leg to address the problem. This was like putting a dagger in me. With RSD, the slightest weight on the leg caused pain. I was a non-functioning person. What did I do to deserve this?

To make matters worse, I was testing some mascara at work, and my eyes blew up. They were so swollen. I worked with mascara for years. I extolled the virtue of mascara making eyes look beautiful. Now mascara made my eyes ugly. I was rushed to an ophthalmologist. I thought I had an allergic reaction to the mascara. It was worse than that. Much worse. I was told I had glaucoma in both eyes. I needed emergency laser surgery. How was this possible? My eye pressure was always good. I wanted to crawl into a hole and stay there. My parents came to the rescue again. They took me to the doctor's for each surgery and brought me home. After the surgery in both eyes, my doctor told me that I was close to nerve blindness. The surgeries saved my vision. Was it possible that God used mascara to get me to the ophthalmologist? If that did not happen, I may never have known that I had glaucoma. The one thing I was sure of was that I was at the point I could not function. I needed to talk with my boss. It was decided that I should go on a three-month disability to give myself time to heal. My physical therapy was switched to a location close to home. I did everything I was supposed to do and was not getting any better. I did not understand what was happening to me. I cried out to God, "Help me!"

I needed to also deal with the fact that I was not feeling well. I needed to get to a general practitioner, but I did not trust doctors. I had two knee surgeries and still could not walk. I had taken medication for years and still was not feeling any better. I decided to go a different route. I was referred to a naturopathic doctor. I made an appointment. It was there that I discovered why these horrific health issues were happening to me. I discovered that the medications I was on for so long for allergies and sinus infections were steroids. They wreaked havoc with my body. I discovered that is why I blew up like a balloon. My grandmother said, "How did you get so big?" It was the steroids. Why was my knee not healing? It was the steroids. I broke down. I cried out for an answer. I now had the answer. I also discovered that my body was damaged. It was going to be a long road back to reverse the effects of the steroids. I discovered that steroids can cause glaucoma. I discovered that steroids could affect the metabolism and thyroid. I discovered steroids can break the body down. I was living in this nightmare. I started to pursue the natural route to my healthcare. Through this process, I learned that I was sensitive to prescription medications. If there were side effects, I got them.

My trust in doctors was non-existent. I realized that I was not even trusting God. It was time to find a church.

I needed to go to church. I called several churches in the area, and only one pastor returned my call. We chatted for a while. I told him I just moved back to New York, and I was dealing with some serious physical challenges. He asked if I could do food shopping for myself. I thought that was a strange question. I answered no. He then said that he and his wife would help me out. He asked me to prepare a grocery list and asked if they could visit after the shopping was done. I was stunned. Never had any church leader offered to help me. We visited for about two hours, and I started attending the church. I was there for eight years. It was a small church, and it was more like a family. Everyone knew everyone. It is just what I needed at the time.

I spent a great deal of time with the Lord. He continued to answer my cry for help. I saw an ad in a local paper for a Miracle Crusade at the Nassau Coliseum on Long Island. I did not know how I was going to get there. It was at least 1 and 1/2 hour drive. It was my right leg that was injured, up to that point, I could only drive for about 15 minutes at a time. It was basically drive to physical therapy and back. I felt a strong prompting to go to the crusade. It was scheduled for Thursday and Friday, but there was a prayer meeting scheduled for the Wednesday evening. I decided to arrive on Wednesday. Not wanting to drive back and forth from Long Island to Tarrytown, I booked a hotel room.

I arrived safely and made it in time for the prayer meeting. This prayer meeting was intense. I had been involved in prayer meetings before but not this level. I am grateful I read the book, Intercession Thrilling and Fulfilling by Joy Dawson. It helped me understand intercessory prayer. My prayer life had intensified. I prayed a lot in my prayer language. I often cried during prayer and did not understand why. I needed to understand. I had grown since I received my prayer language and said to the pastor, "If it's the devil, why do I want to pray more." I have a need to pray. Scripture says to pray without ceasing. I did.

I planned to sit in my chair and pray quietly. Once again, God had a different plan. The atmosphere was charged with the presence of the Holy Spirit. I started shaking all over. My right leg started shaking. I could not control it. Then, I started praying aloud in my prayer language. It did not sound like Italian. It sounded like Russian. I had no idea what I was praying. One of the leaders came over to me to see what was going on. She encouraged me to let it out. Let it out I did. I do not know how long that lasted. What was God doing? I just know I felt like a wet noodle when it was over. I just wanted to go to bed.

I managed to attend the crusade on Thursday and enjoyed the worship and preaching. Then, I went to the service on Friday morning.

There were probably 20,000 people in attendance. I was directed to a seat up front to the left of the stage. I got lost in the worship. Tears streamed down my face as I worshipped the Lord. Suddenly, I started shaking again. I felt a tremendous heat going through my body. I was lifted off my feet and fell into the row in front of me. I was helped up and I started jumping up and down. There was no way I could do that. I got out of the row and started running up and down the stairs. Again, there was no way I could do that. One of the ushers realized I was experiencing a healing and came over to me. Before I knew it, I was ushered out of the auditorium and brought backstage. I was still shaking. I was brought into the medical room. The doctors asked me questions. I explained what physical challenges I had and now I did not. They examined me and declared that I had received a healing. I was then escorted back into the auditorium and soon found myself on the stage. The next thing I knew I was standing on the stage talking to Pastor Benny Hinn and giving my testimony. He then said, "Touch," and I was slain in the spirit right there on the stage. I was helped up and went back to my seat. I continued to feel heat for hours. For days, I tried to wrap my head around what happened to me.

The week after my miracle, I received a follow up call from the ministry. They wanted to see how I was doing. I explained the changes I was seeing and how I was now able to walk and do things I could not do before. They advised me to pace myself. I did receive my healing, but it was wise to take it slow. I was healed in the spiritual realm, but my body needed to catch up in the natural realm. For one year, I could not do my physical therapy without pain. Now I was able to do the exercises and within six weeks my knee was strong again. I could do stairs. I could walk. I learned I had to fight to keep my healing. One day I drove to physical therapy. When I got out of the car, I could not walk. I was in pain. I became a warrior. I knew I was healed. No demon in hell could take it from me. I got back in my car. The battle began. I prayed in the spirit. I declared healing scriptures. I worshipped the Lord. I declared my healing. I would not let up. The battle was so intense my car was shaking. After twenty minutes, I knew the battle was over. I got out of my car, walked into physical therapy without pain. I was no longer a victim. I was victorious!

On June 26, 1997, I received my miracle. I was advised to get medical documentation confirming my miracle. In August, I had an appointment with the orthopedic surgeon. After examining me, he said, "Claudia, I like to be honest. I can't explain what happened to you." I said, "I can. I believe in the power of prayer. God answers prayer. God stepped in." He had that look of this person is crazy, but then again, he could not explain my miraculous turnaround.

God did not disappoint. I was excited to go back to work and redeem myself. I kept in touch with my boss throughout this ordeal. When I spoke to him that I was ready to come back, he coldly told me, "You don't have a job to come back to." I was speechless. "What?" "You're laid off." End of conversation. That was it. I sat in my living room in stunned silence. Just then, my doorbell rang. I got up to answer it, and it was a delivery man with a basket of goodies from the president of my ad agency welcoming me back. In the basket, was a tape of a commercial we worked on together that was another home run. In my shock, I called her. I thanked her for the gift. I then explained that I was just told I no longer had a job. She was livid. She assured me she would do everything in her power to help me get situated into a new position. She kept her word. I was not alone.

Chapter 7

A Hard Look in the Mirror

Over the years, I have been the poster child for the definition of insanity. I kept doing the same thing over again expecting a different result. I worked years in the corporate roller coaster. Up to this point, I had been laid off more than once, I experienced a workplace injury and was on disability and was miraculously healed. Yet, I continued to work around the clock and was exhausted. I kept pursuing the elusive corporate success story. I wanted to climb the corporate ladder with the goal of becoming a Vice President of Marketing. Would I ever learn that this was not for me? It took several more years of being the hamster in the wheel going around in circles. I was so programmed that this was what I had to do to be considered successful. I had blinders on and could not see that I was force fitting myself into the universal idea of success.

I needed to take a hard look at myself. My sister always told me that I was my own worst critic. I would beat myself up with every mistake. I did not understand that life was a process with many lessons along the way. The key was to learn from the mistakes. I was wired so tightly and was always on a mission to get the job done. It was all about performance. If I did a good job, I would get rewarded. If not, I would be punished. My childhood insecurities loomed large. As I was about to embark on another link in my corporate resume, my confidence was low. I acted like I was confident, but inside I was trembling.

I had some growth in challenging authority, but my problem with authority was evident. I still carried the misguided notion that authority figures were always right. That is why they were in positions of authority. Even though I became more skilled at managing people, I still struggled with managing up. I was in an emotional boxing match with myself. I had an opinion and wanted to be heard, yet I withdrew when I was challenged by my bosses. I did not realize they were just asking questions to better understand my thought process and recommendations. I thought they were attacking me. I felt stupid and was back in the dumb row. Being a guppy in a sea of sharks was not exactly the formula for success.

The scripture John 10:10 (AMP) says, "The thief comes only in order to steal and kill and destroy. I came that they may have and enjoy life, and have it in abundance [to the full, till it overflows]." What was this abundant life? I knew I was not enjoying life. I was grateful I was walking, but my body still needed a complete overhaul. I suffered terribly with allergies. I battled to lose weight. I felt beaten up and was tentative about moving forward. I felt alone and I tended to look at the glass half empty instead of half full. A close friend once told me, "You're like a dog who keeps getting kicked, but you keep getting up." The good part is I keep getting up. The bad part is I did not know how to fight. I think my personality was a combination of my mother and father. My mother was negative and worried about everything. My father took life in stride and had a positive attitude. Unfortunately, I tended to lean toward the negative. I was a contradiction. The simplest things give me joy, yet I focused on material things. I like to gather facts and make educated decisions quickly, yet I tended to question my decisions. I love the arts, yet I focused on work and had little time to enjoy what gave me pleasure. I needed to express myself on many levels, but I shut my voice down. After all, who would want to listen to someone who is stupid.

I realized that I was battling myself. I could not hide from myself. I came to the harsh reality that I did not like myself. I put myself on the defensive and pushed people away. I was sending out signals. The wrong kind of signals. This was most true in my personal life. I grew up believing I would marry and have children. That is what girls did. For me, that would not happen. I have never been in love. I have never even been in like. Being around men made me uncomfortable.

I did not have a healthy understanding of male/female relationships. My role model should have been my parents, but it was not. I remember a lot of arguing. One specific night stands out. I was at the impressionable age of nine years old. My sister and I were in our bedroom, and I could hear my parents arguing. My father was heading out to go to the Knights of Columbus. My mother complained that he was never home. She wanted him to spend time with her. My father, aka Mt. Vesuvius, erupted. I thought they were going to come to blows. I hid in my room shaking. My sister tried to keep me calm. The fight got so bad that my aunt came upstairs to intervene. My father would have none of it. My aunt came into our bedroom and took my sister and me downstairs. There was no consoling me. I was sure my parents were going to get divorced. I knew my father loved us. I knew he loved me. Yet, I believe my father's temper planted a seed that caused me to be afraid of men. I did not want to do anything that would set him off. Looking back, I think all that fighting soured me on marriage. I built a wall that screamed DON'T TOUCH.

Amazingly, my parents were married for 61 years. In all those years, I remember the arguing, but I do not remember any displays of affection.

There may have been a hug or a kiss, but that was about it. I often wondered if they loved each other. When I was older, I asked my mother about it. She said, "That is reserved for the bedroom." The arguing and that sense of propriety had an impact on me. I stiffened when I was around men. When my parents were married about 58 years, we were visiting my sister. I watched my parents as they sat on the sofa. I saw my mother and father holding hands, and they just looked in each other's eyes. I never saw them do that before. Later in the day, I asked my mother about it. She looked at me and said, "I know your father loves me." I had to take that in and then said, "What do you mean?" She explained, "Since I have not been well, he has taken care of me. He even takes me to church every week without complaint. He would not do that if he did not love me." My eyes filled up with tears. I hugged her. It was beautiful and sad at the same time. It was beautiful because my father was finally talking her love language which was acts of service. It meant everything to her. It was sad because it took 58 years of marriage for her to realize her husband loved her.

At ten, I became uncomfortable with me. I became a "young lady." I did not understand what was happening to me. I thought I was dying. My sister was older and realized I was no longer a little girl. She called for my mother. My mother showed me what to do and then she gave me a book. I read the book and still did not understand about the birds and the bees. I could only focus on the fact that I was in a great deal of pain each month. Then, overnight, I went from being flat chested to curvaceous. In a time when Twiggy was all the rage, I physically did not fit in. I felt fat. My mother did not understand why I felt that way. My mother was curvaceous, and my dad would call her Zsa after Zsa Zsa Gabor. She loved it. It affirmed that she was beautiful. For me thin was in which meant I was out. To make matters worse, my sister was tall and thin. My mother would make malteds for her to fatten her up. She was still thin. It did not matter that I took after my mom and my dad thought she was beautiful. It did not matter that Marilyn Monroe was considered one of the sexiest women in the world. It mattered that I was not skinny. My self-image was low. I hated being a girl.

At 16, I was in a hygiene class and the teacher presented a slide show of how babies are made. I was mortified. Even though I read that book at ten years old, I knew nothing. Like I said, I grew up in the backyard. I could not handle the thought of my parents doing that. I withdrew. My dad noticed I was quiet, and he asked me about it. I said the proverbial, "Nothing." He knew better. He finally got me to explain what was bothering me. The unthinkable happened. My father explained life to me. This should have been my mother. But she gave me a book. At least I got a book. My grandmother told my mother to stay away from boys. If she could not talk about it, how could my father. He always managed to get me to tell him what was on my mind. He often challenged my sister and me to think for ourselves and justify our opinions. This was not opinion. This was fact. This was the ultimate. Would I make him angry if I told him I was embarrassed? I remember only one time my father was angry with me. I purchased a pair of shoes at a department store in downtown Brooklyn. When I brought them home, I realized I had the wrong size. I needed to return them. My dad did not want me to take the train, so he volunteered to drive me. It was about an hour drive with traffic. We enjoyed the drive together. When we arrived at the store, I realized I forgot to take the shoes with me. I could feel the cold chill start to form in the car. My dad did not say anything. He just looked at me with an icy stare. The silence was deafening on the ride home. When we arrived, through gritted teeth, my father said, "Get the shoes." What? "Get the shoes." I looked at him.

I gulped. Then, I ran into the house and got my shoes. He drove me all the way back to the store to return them. It was a quiet ride there and back. When we arrived home, all I could do was throw my arms around him and say, "Thank you, Daddy." His hug back was heartfelt. Deep down I knew my dad would not yell at me if I felt embarrassed. I was the one who was uncomfortable. He was relaxed. I squirmed. Here I am his "leetle one" and he was sharing all this taboo information with me. We did not talk about such things. It was time. He explained things in a way I would understand. I felt safe and embarrassed at the same time. He took it in stride.

All of this had an impact on me. I did not date at all. I was that good little Catholic girl. I was shy and dressed modestly, I wore button down blouses, and I made sure that top button was buttoned. I could not risk showing cleavage. I had my first date when I turned eighteen. I was introduced to him by a friend, and we went out once. Just once. It was around my birthday. I did not know my family was planning a surprise party for me, and when he came to pick me up, my sister called me out of the room. I thought that was strange. I did not want to leave him alone with my parents. I left the room, and in my absence, my parents invited him to the party. I think that scared him off. We did not even have our date yet. I remember he was distant during our date. When I found out that my parents invited him to my party, I was upset. How dare they embarrass me like that? No wonder the date was awkward. No wonder he never called again. I did have another date, though, on my 18th birthday. My dad took me to dinner and a Broadway show. At the time, I did not know it was a ruse to get me out of the house. When we returned home, Surprise! After that date with my dad, it became a tradition every year. My dad would take me to dinner and the theater. I picked the restaurant and the show. It was my birthday. It was my choice. There is a saying that girls look for husbands like their dads. My dad had qualities I would look for in a husband. He was strong. He had integrity. He kept his word. He was a good provider. His family came first. He loved us. He loved me. He spent time with me. He made me feel special.

At 21, I attended a bible study at the Catholic church I attended. There was a priest teaching the class. He started to teach on original sin. I remember it as if it were yesterday. He said, "Original sin was not an apple from a tree, but a pair on the ground." That is the day it forever registered with me that sex was sin. He did not explain that sex outside of marriage was sin. I was confused. You mean my parents were sinning! Did they have to go to confession. As my understanding of scripture increased, I realized that the Lord created sex and said in Genesis 9:7 NKJV) "…be fruitful and multiply…" I learned that sex is not a sin within the sanctity of marriage. Even though I had a warped understanding of sex, that made sense to me.

Not having that special someone in my life did not stop me from having a life. I traveled. I worked in corporate America. I danced. I met men, but they were friends. Men just were not interested in me romantically. The wall I built worked. This was a painful reality when I was on vacation. I met a man and he said, in no uncertain terms, "You don't need a man." He saw me as this independent woman who made a good living. He thought a man should make the decisions and be the provider. I held it together. When we were dancing, I sent him a message that was loud and clear. He asked me what I wanted to do that evening. I played coy and said, "Oh, I'm not sure. Why don't you decide." He just looked at me. He said, "What are you doing?" I said, "What do you mean?" He recognized that I was not the demure woman he wanted. It was the 1980's. I was a feminist who was an independent woman in an army of sisters breaking through the glass ceiling. I did not need a man to support me financially. I needed a man to love me. When I acted indecisive and coy, he then said, "Stop it. That is not you." I said, "Exactly! A woman does not need a man just for financial support." In that moment, I knew who I was. I left him on the dance floor. I walked away and did not turn back. I called a male friend of mine when I returned home. I needed his opinion if I gave out the vibe that I do not need a man. He told me the guy was a jerk.

Another opportunity presented itself. I met a man while I was cruising the Caribbean. We hit it off. He filled the man of my dreams criteria. He was a successful entrepreneur and had his own plane. We had a wonderful time snorkeling and visiting different sights. We kept in touch after vacation ended. He lived in the Albany NY area flew to NYC for the 100th year anniversary celebration of the Brooklyn Bridge. We had a wonderful weekend. There were so many things happening in the city culminating with the fireworks display at the Brooklyn Bridge.

After he returned home, we never spoke to each other again. What happened? I can only surmise. Hotels rooms were hard to come by. I had my own apartment, and I offered to have him stay at my place. I felt it would not be right for me to be in the apartment with him. I was an anomaly. In a culture of sexual freedom, I knew who I was. I would not compromise that I believed in waiting until marriage. If I stayed at my apartment, I would send the wrong signal. I respected myself. I wanted him to respect me. I stayed at my parents. I did not question my moral compass. It was me. I understood it. I did not understand how to be a woman. In my naivete, I did not know how to keep him interested, while being true to myself. I had no experience. I had no teacher. I am still learning.

In Connecticut, I joined a dating network for singles. It was obvious that I needed help. I filled out the application. I spoke with the consultant assigned to me. I explained the qualities I was looking for in a man. I was excited with the possibility that I would meet someone. I met someone. And another. And another. And another. There were many "only one night" dates. I did not know why I bothered to fill out an application and meet with the consultant. I had nothing in common with the men I met. There was only once exception. I did have four dates with one guy. That was a record. In four dates, I wondered if he found me attractive. He was a perfect gentleman. We did not even hold hands until date four. Was that normal? I did not know what was normal or not? Then, something unexpected happened. I received my first kiss. Somehow, I knew it was coming. I had seen enough movies. Miraculously, I did not pull away. For the first time, I was in a man's arms. This was a new dance. I let him lead. He was gentle. I felt safe. Even so, I knew I did not want to pursue a relationship with him. In getting to know him, I realized he was cheap. I do not mind if a man is frugal, but cheap is another matter. That did not work for me. Also, I was not a true feminist. I expected a man to open a car door for me and pull out my chair. That is what my father did. That is what I expected. I did not have the foresight to understand that I could let him know these things mattered to me. The deal breaker was that he also had a cat. I could not get near a cat without having a severe allergic reaction. I could not get near him. My first kiss was my only kiss.

In Memphis, I had male friends. After church on Sunday evenings, we would usually go out as a group to get a bite to eat. One night, it was just one friend and me. As we chatted, he started telling me about this woman at church that he was interested in. He was going on with his tale of woe. They were both divorced more than once, and he was not sure if she was ready for another relationship. I listened and moved into a slow boil. I had been through this before. Did I have therapist emblazoned across my forehead? I am not a therapist. I am the forever friend. I lived through male friends having problems with their significant others and dumping on me. There is one glaring example. When I received my MBA, I invited friends over to my apartment to celebrate before we headed into the city to dance the night away. A dear friend was engaged. I had never met his fiancé. She made quite an impression. She blasted into my apartment like a whirlwind, plopped herself on my sofa and started bemoaning what I served. She then announced she did not like the club I chose to go to that night. This was my night. I looked at my friend, and to keep the peace, we went to the club she suggested. It was a nightmare. I hated the club. I hated the music. I hated that my special evening was turned upside down. My friends saw I was upset. They were too. They offered to drive me home. I left my dear friend and his fiancé at the club. He called me the next day to apologize. I told him, in no uncertain terms, "I don't ever want to be in the same room with her. What do you see in her? She is walking all over you! I tell you right now, I am not attending your wedding. There is no way I can act like I believe you two belong together." I hung up. Her true colors came out. Six weeks later, he broke off the engagement. I stood by him, and we are friends to this day. With such a history, I did not want to hear it. As my friend continued to dump his love troubles on me, I boiled over. I started to cry and said, "I'm so sick and tired of men telling me about their romantic troubles. What is wrong with me? Why aren't men interested in me?" I soon realized I created an uncomfortable situation. This was the South. Men in the restaurant started to get up to come to my aid. They must have thought I was being abused. I just raised my hand and indicated I was okay. I completely shocked my friend. I shocked me. He did not know what to say. We did not get together again, after that. I cannot blame him.

In New York, I thought about going on internet dating. It was a new concept at the time. One Sunday morning, I was watching a minister on Christian television. He was preaching. Suddenly, he looked straight into the camera and said, "There's a woman out there who is thinking about going on internet dating. The Lord says, "Don't you dare!" Then he went back to preaching. I was learning how to hear the voice of God. There was no doubt that the Lord spoke to me loud and clear. The fear of God hit me. I did not understand men. At times, I did not understand myself. In that moment, I understood the Lord. I felt He protected me. I obeyed. I never went on internet dating.

Looking in the mirror is hard. I had to deal with me. I went for pastoral counseling. I prayed. I cried out to God. It has been one foot in front of the other. It has not been easy, but through self-reflection, I realized there were positives within the negatives. I have learned that when people have experienced a great deal of rejection, they can try to buy love. I was no exception. I was and still am a giver. I get great joy in giving to others. If I can touch someone or put a smile on someone's face, I get a smile too. This is especially true with children. I love kids. One Sunday morning, the pastor's wife announced they needed volunteers for the nursery. I felt I should volunteer but I threw out the fleece. I thought if she announced it again next week, I would volunteer. Well, she did. I took a deep breath after service and went up to talk to her. I started to cry. I burst out with, "I want to volunteer for the nursery, but I don't know nothin' about birthin' no babies." She laughed and said I should not be concerned about it. I hoped she was right. I have so much love to give. I hoped the babies would receive my love and I could receive their unconditional love back.

She did not know that I had a history of not knowing what to do when it came to babies. When my niece was born. I told my sister I would babysit when she turned three months old. I felt there was more substance to a baby at three months old. I did put a condition on my love. I told my sister that I would not change a poopy diaper. She looked at me and said, "I have no control over that." Well, the three-month mark arrived, and I kept my promise. My sister filled me in on all the details. I was ready. Then, lo and behold, before my sister and brother-in-law left for their evening out, my niece deposited a present in her diaper. I said, "Oh Sis…" My sister looked at me and in disbelief said, "You're not really going to ask me to change her diaper." I had that Cheshire cat smile and said, "An agreement is an agreement." My sister gave me that long glare. She put on an apron and changed the baby's diaper. Later that evening, I was feeding my niece her bottle, tears welled up in me as I lovingly watched her drink her bottle while she slept. Her little arm and hand were around me and rested on my back. It hit me that she trusted me unconditionally. I did not trust myself.

I learned there is payback. In the nursery, there was one baby boy who was a regular. His mother dropped him off along with his food and a change of clothes if necessary. They were necessary. Within minutes after feeding him his bottle, he had an epic flow in his diaper. What a mess! What I could not do for my niece, I did for him. I put his needs before mine. I showed him unconditional love. I brought him into the bathroom to wash him down. I changed his clothes and breathed a sigh of relief. Then, a repeat performance. I thought I was going to be sick. I went through the whole thing again only this time I was having trouble dressing him. His nine-year old sister was watching the whole event. She stepped in and saved me. She pointed out that I was putting the baby's clothes on backwards. A nine-year old knew more about taking care of a baby than I did. After the service was finished, his mother came to the nursery to pick him up. She told me that the baby had been constipated. I looked at her with my death stare and matter-of-factly said, "Not anymore." As horrible as it was, I was relieved that I survived. I am grateful he did too.

I worked in the nursery for two years. After that, I was moved to working with the children. I started out as a teacher's assistant and then was promoted to Sunday School teacher. My first day as an Assistant did not start out well. Before service, I participated in morning prayer. I did not understand why things happened to me when I prayed. I tended to pray with fervor. I would sometimes cry. I would sometimes shake. I knew it was not me. These manifestations would only happen when I prayed and when I worshipped. After prayer finished, my pastor's wife pulled me aside and chastened me for the way I prayed. I was told I needed to be careful and to stop it. I looked at her in disbelief. I wanted to scream, "Are you kidding me? You're telling me I don't pray right?" Instead, I quenched my voice. She was the Pastor's wife. She was authority. I turned and walked away. I started to cry. Then, I realized this is not about me. I made a commitment. The children needed me. I needed them. We needed each other.

I loved on the children, but I was firm. I guess all the discipline I received growing up affected on me. However, I would never humiliate a child. If discipline was needed, I would do so privately and without any yelling. I lowered my voice an octave. I am amazed at how effective it is. There was one young boy in the class. His parents called him a wild child, and he fit the bill. It is as if they labeled him. He was misbehaving. I quietly went behind him, bent down and whispered, "We can discuss your behavior here or we can go outside. Your choice." He knew I meant business. That wild child calmed down very quickly. Even though I was a disciplinarian, the children responded well to me. They looked forward to when it was my week to teach. Parents always knew when it was my week. The children got excited and were involved in each lesson. What started out as tragedy turned into triumph. I was learning how to balance discipline with love.

The children accepted me for who I am. That was important to me. I did not have to perform for them. I just had to give my time and myself to them. I felt fulfilled. On the flip side of being a giver, this kind of personality trait attracted people who were takers which led to a lot of hurt and disappointment. I was used, abused, lied to, and pummeled in relationships.

I later realized these people were co-dependent. Whenever something was wrong in the relationship, the blame was fully put on me. I would immediately ask, "What did I do wrong?" I craved friendship. I took all the responsibility. I realized I only spoke up when I was pushed to my limit. Anger became my voice. I would stuff everything inside until I exploded.

I became very cynical. Trusting people became non-existent. I wanted to trust people. I learned not to. This made it difficult to trust God. I had experienced miracles in my life. I walked closer with the Lord, but trust was a major hurdle for me. I look back and laugh when people said, "Just trust God." It is not that easy. I trusted myself and did not ask for help. Honestly, I did not ask for anything. I felt I was not worth it. I think everyone knows the saying, "God helps those who help themselves." That is not biblical. I needed to learn to depend on

God. It was a long road complete with kicking, screaming, tantrums and facing inward pain. I thought this was supposed to be simpler than I was taught.

The simple part is that Jesus died for my sins, and all I had to do was ask Him into my heart. The rest was hard. The scripture says, "Whoever wants to be my disciple must deny themselves and take up their cross daily and follow me." (Luke 9:23, NIV). I had to learn that the Lord is relentless in character refinement. I had to be willing to change. I had to be willing to let go of the past. I had to learn that He loves me. I had to learn that He does have an abundant life for me. This was a big part of my problem. I did not believe God loved me unconditionally. For me, love was performance based. I felt if I did not get things right, I would be punished. I continued to trust myself. Yet, in my brokenness, I was serious when I cried out for God to help me. I needed to face my weaknesses. I needed to face my fears. I needed to come face to face with me. Yet in my desperation, I fought God. Why could I not trust Him unconditionally the way my niece trusted me unconditionally as she slept peacefully in my arms. Was my childhood fear of God being angry with me overriding what I was learning about Him?

My fear of being punished by God flowed over into my relationship with the pastors of my Church. The pastor of the church I attended was, without question, a strong personality. He knew what he believed, and the scriptures were the undisputed word of God. I attended the church for eight years and was consumed with the word of God every week. I needed to know what God said about things and about me. I learned how to read the scriptures and how to apply them to my life. He and his wife were patient with me as they recognized I needed much healing. In my fear of authority, I felt they were forceful in their approach. They were like parents who showed love but believed in discipline. I knew that all my life. I accepted and resisted it at the same time. They encouraged me in my walk with the Lord and in the spiritual gifts that were evident in me. Yet, there were many circumstances that just fed into my feeling of inadequacy.

I was dealing with the fallout from the steroids, and I struggled physically. I was laid off from work, financially struggling and fighting a legal battle because of the layoff. I was emotionally spiraling downward. The pastor kept telling me to speak the word of God. Let it get into your spirit. I remember saying, "I'm trying, but it doesn't seem to work." I was at my lowest. I struggle to confess this, but I was having thoughts of ending it all. I wanted to end all the pain. Yet, deep inside, I still had that fight to keep going. I knew I could not go through with it. One Sunday, there was a special guest speaker. He taught on Samson and described him as one of the only heroes of the bible who committed suicide. It is so hard to say that word. He knew that by pulling down the pillars of the temple he would be killed. The minister talked about despair and about hope. He then said, "If anyone has ever thought of committing suicide, to come up for prayer and ministry." No one made a move. How could anyone admit to such horrible thoughts? After what felt like an eternity, I felt a tugging within to go up to the altar. I fought that feeling. I finally relented. As I did, I felt a strength within me that propelled each step forward. When I got to the altar, I felt all eyes were boring into the back of my skull. I felt humiliated for being so weak and desperate for love at the same time. I needed love and compassion. Instead, the pastor's wife took me aside and said, "We can't let you prophesy. You're too broken." I had to look up. I realized this was between me and God. Every day exposed new revelations and realities. Every day brought new challenges and hope. Every day tested my metal and my faith. I have learned that every day is an opportunity to grow or recede. I chose to grow. I chose to have hope. I chose to move forward.

Chapter 8
The Next Phase

My primary focus was to find a new job. I mentioned that the president of my ad agency kept her word. She wrote letters of introduction for me to the presidents of companies and was quite laudatory in her letters. The head of creative at the agency also came to my assistance. She highly recommended me to the president of Revlon. I left Revlon because I felt it was not real marketing and I worked around the clock. Why would I go back? It had been ten years and I still had a bad taste in my mouth. Should I have taken that as a sign? I was conflicted. I respected my former creative director and welcomed her help. I needed a job, but I did not want to make another mistake. I decided to keep an open mind. Even though I was grateful for the connection, I needed to do my homework. I contacted those I knew in the industry who would give me their honest opinion. My research showed that the company had turned around.

It was the recession of 1997, and many times, I was told that I would never get a position at the level I was at before. I was told I would probably have to take a step back and a pay cut. That was disheartening. I did not want to go backwards. I was grateful for the foot in the door, but I did not leave it there. I kept my head down and followed-up on introductions. I worked with executive recruiters. I tenaciously followed up on every lead. Only the door to Revlon stayed open. For four months, I spoke once a week to the gatekeeper for the president of Revlon. My follow up would lead to chats with her and then, extended conversations. The day finally arrived when I was brought in for a formal interview. I learned that the company was restructuring, and they wanted me to interview for the Director of Marketing on the Almay eye business. My experience at Maybelline was the perfect fit. I went through the interview process and was offered the position of

Director of Eyes for Almay at more pay than I had before. I felt this was a sign. It was the same sign I received when I was offered the job at Maybelline. I breathed a sigh of relief that I was on the right track.

I was on the job for three weeks and settling in. Then, I was informed that I was being moved over to be Director of the Almay Face and Treatment business. This was like a repeat performance of my Director on the Nail Business at Revlon resigning a week after I started. Did the company turnaround or was it more of the same? Was I fed a line? I bit my tongue and accepted the change. I now needed to settle in on the Face and Treatment business. My first day on the job, I was met with a personnel issue that thwarted easing into the job. I arrived at 8:30 a.m. The assistant on the face business was perched at my office door. She introduced herself and asked if she could meet with me. I had not even put my key in the door to my new office. I invited her in. It was obvious she was upset. I let her speak. I listened. She shared how difficult it was to work with the manager on the business. She gave me example after example to substantiate her claim. I digested what she said and thanked her for sharing her concerns with me. I explained that I would need to assess the situation to be able to determine of how best to handle things. I said I needed about three weeks. She nodded in agreement. She no sooner left my office when the manager came flying in the door. She closed the door, sat down, and started railing against the assistant. I noticed something had changed. I did not have to establish myself as the director. I was the Director. I kept my cool. They reported to me. I told her the same thing I told the assistant. I would need three weeks to assess the situation.

The next three weeks were difficult. I was up to the challenge. I prayed for wisdom. I did my homework. I started to ask support groups about each member of my team. I set up meetings with both the manager and the assistant. I wanted to assess how they worked together and individually. The manager was never available. She was either out sick or had some other reason for not being there. Instead, she called me when I was on a business trip. She railed against the assistant manager. Ice water ran through my veins. In no uncertain terms, I told her I would discuss this with her when I returned. I tested the waters to see whose version of events was accurate. I realized that the assistant was telling the truth and flourished as I gave her the opportunity to show her stuff. The three weeks were up. I knew what I needed to do.

I expected people to do their jobs with excellence. I rewarded jobs well done, and I disciplined when necessary. My management style was firm but fair. I did not tolerate any nonsense. In the three weeks, I listened. I gathered information. I came to an educated decision. I silenced other voices and listened to my own voice. I needed to speak to my management to deal with the manager. She was a disturbing force on my team and with others. I was too late. The manager went around me and spoke to management first. She complained about me and said I was not handling things well. I had a heart to heart with management. I revealed what I had learned in three weeks and voiced my opinion that the manager was a problem. They agreed that something needed to be done. It was at that moment I learned that bad behavior was often rewarded. Those who stomped their feet and threw tantrums were often placated. I felt the manager needed to be disciplined. My Senior Vice President informed that they were promoting her to the Senior Manager position on a smaller business. Excuse me! I said I believed that this decision should have been discussed with me first. I realized this battle was over. I had grown. I knew what battles to fight and which ones to let go. On the bright side, the manager was off my team. I replaced her with another individual who I felt would be a better fit. The assistant and my new manager hit it off. Within a few months, the assistant blossomed and demonstrated her affinity for the job. I promoted her to an associate within six months.

I found my footing within the company. My expertise came through. I was able to develop new strategies for the business and oversaw successful new product launches. Then a new test presented itself. There was another director on the Almay team who was on the Lip and Nail business. Almay was facing the introduction of two major brands that posed significant competition to the face business. It was determined that we needed to do a full analysis of the competition and make strategic recommendations on how to thwart their entry into the market. The Director of Lip and Nail cut me off in that meeting and volunteered to do the analysis. I just looked at her and remained stunned. That all too familiar knot formed in my stomach. I was so strong dealing with my subordinates, why am I so weak when I concerns me? I did not know what to say. I had a momentary panic that I was being undermined. Thoughts flashed through my mind. How dare she? This is my business. What do I do? I just looked at the Executive Vice President. She returned my gaze and intervened. She said that my team should do the recon since our business would be the most affected. I felt relieved and unnerved at the same time. I put pressure on myself. I needed to really prove myself on this project.

It took weeks to pull the analysis together. I oversaw the entire project and made sure it was thorough and answered questions people would not even think to ask. This was the first time I felt good about my work without the approval from others. I lit up. I had taken a step back to listen to that still small voice within me. That listening gave me the confidence that I knew what I was doing. When we were finished, I reviewed the entire presentation with my team. The final touch was my executive summary. We first presented to both my Vice President and Senior Vice President. I gave every member on the team a piece of the action. It was well received, and every question was answered. When I emerged from the meeting, I was surprised to see the Director of Lip and Nail lurking around outside. She was dying to know how the meeting went. I think she secretly wanted me to fail. I did not realize that she was jealous and insecure. Next, we presented the plan to the Executive Vice President and then the President of the company.

Our analysis and recommendations were spot on, and we put the plan into action. I succeeded. I proved myself. We read the competition correctly and were able to successfully curtail their entrée into the industry. One company even pulled their products from the market within the first year. I passed the test. Or so I thought.

Other challenges surfaced. Each marketing team was to do a complete analysis of their business and make recommendations. Each presentation followed an agreed upon format. The Director of the Revlon Face business and myself disagreed. We felt the format was more surface than substance. We decided to do our own format. The day of the presentations arrived. Everyone was in the main conference room together with management including the President of the company. I sat there all day. I listened to the questions asked by management. They were the same questions that went unanswered from presentation to presentation. It was now our turn. There was a hushed silence as others recognized that our presentation was different. It was nerve wracking, but we were prepared. We answered every question to their satisfaction. When we finished, the president leaned over to me and said how pleased she was with our presentation and recommendations. She did not do that with anyone else. The Executive Vice President was stunned. I was grateful things went well, but no one else was. The claws came out and jealously reared its ugly head. Even though I recognized it, I still believed I would be accepted. I was wrong.

The longer I worked for the company, I felt things were not quite right. I not only had to swim through a sea the sharks, but I also struggled to understand the heavy shipments of products at the end of each quarter. Every time I asked questions, I never got an answer. I had a gnawing feeling in my stomach. It was not fear. I did not know it was my spiritual gift of discernment stirring within me. Things started to deteriorate. My direct superior, the Vice President resigned soon followed by the resignation of the Senior Vice President. That should have been a clear sign. As one of the senior members of the marketing team, I tried to step up and guide the ship. Others would not let that happen. There was conflict and infighting. People vied to become the next Vice President. Management brought in a new Senior Vice President. She had worked at the company before. Once again, I felt I needed to prove myself. We did not hit it off. She made it a point to leave me out of meetings. Spiritually, I was growing, but I believed I needed to perform for God to love me. Emotionally, I felt overlooked. Physically, I was still dealing with the fallout from the steroids. I tore a tendon in my right ankle and had to wear a removable ankle cast. I could only wear sneakers because the cast would not fit in regular shoes. My new boss was not happy. I tried to explain, but this was a beauty company and image was everything. My sneakers were my missing tooth. She did not see me. She only saw the sneakers. During this time, my manager was promoted to a Senior Manager on another business. I brought in a new manager and a new administrative assistant. I worked around the clock. Leaving at 6:30 pm was considered working a half day. Her attitude toward me caused my dream of being promoted to the Vice President position to disappear. She brought in someone else. Again, I was at ground zero. What did I need to do to move up?

I was given the ultimate test. I was disheartened and I had a bad attitude. I wanted to leave the company. I put out feelers, but nothing materialized. My new boss and I were at odds. I did the unthinkable. I became what I despised. I acted like a petulant child who stomped her feet until she got what she wanted. It worked for everyone else. It did not work for me. He wanted to meet with me. I did not want to meet with him. I knew the conversation that was coming, and I was not ready for it. I did not present myself well. He was not happy. I asked if we could end the meeting and regroup again on Monday. He agreed. It was a rough weekend. I prayed and I asked the Lord to help me. I did not expect what came next. The Lord dealt with my character. I was supposed to be setting the standard not lowering myself the ways of the world. I looked at the outside. God looked at the inside. I needed to be accepted which caused me to look to people instead of the Lord. God needed to deal with the rejection. I needed to be in control. God needed to teach me to trust Him. Just as the apostle Paul had a thorn in his flesh, this was mine. It was not my health. It was not finances. It was my need to be in control. It was the lynchpin that needed to be released so I could trust God instead of myself.

On Monday, I showed up on time for my meeting with my boss. I told him I would like to say something. He sat back and had a tense look on his face. I surprised him. I apologized for my behavior and my attitude. I told him there was no excuse for it. I said I would like to start fresh and work with him. His whole body relaxed. He told me he expected the worst. He thanked me for the apology, and he received my olive branch. I realized that I did not move me back to Revlon for a job. I moved back to get a good look at myself. I needed to change. I learned I could not do it alone.

I felt I took a major step forward spiritually. I listened to that still small voice within me, and I humbled myself not only before God but before a man. For someone who needed to feel accepted that was not easy. I was obedient so I checked the box in performing for God. I still was not in a place where I trusted Him. I no sooner learned this lesson; the bottom fell out of the company. My instincts were right. The stock plummeted almost overnight from $60 per share to $15 per share. So much for stock options. So much for research. Panic set in. People who were with the company for 25 to 30 years no longer had pensions. Savings were wiped out. People were laid off. Those who were not terminated headed for the exits. There was a mass exodus. Myself included.

I learned a lesson, but it was short lived. I did not take time to step back and look at things. I did not allow myself to digest the lesson I learned. I did not pray or take the time to check in with the Lord. I focused on getting a job. Would I ever learn? I interviewed and accepted the position of Director of Color Cosmetics at Avon. One of the highlights of accepting this position was that I was offered a sign on bonus which I would receive after six months. That sign on bonus was a sign that I made it. It was a symbol that I fit in and was accepted. I looked at the outside and the carrot that was dangled in front of me. The company had a great reputation, and my experience was acknowledged. Within my first two weeks, I had a big win. I suggested that the biggest promotion of the year needed more visual impact in the catalogue. That simple suggestion of calling attention to the sale blew sales out of the water. It was nice to have such a win and it emphasized why I was hired.

Things looked good on the business side, but not the personnel side. I made it a policy to get to know each member of my team. I set up individual meetings with each person. I made it a point to sit beside the person on the opposite side of my desk. I wanted the conversation to be comfortable. I later learned that this made quite an impact on one team member. It signaled to her that I was approachable. But there is always one. I met with one of the managers. She quickly informed me that she should be promoted to the open Senior Marketing Manager position. If anyone understood what it was like to prove herself to a new manager, it was me. I listened to her and thanked her for letting me know how she felt. I explained I needed to get to know her and her work. The next day I received a call from my boss, the Vice President of Color Cosmetics. She informed me that this manager made an appointment to see her. She wanted to know if I knew anything about it. I said I had a good idea and explained. She said I should join the meeting since the manager now reported to me. I arrived for the meeting before the manager. She was shocked to see me there. My boss explained that since the manager now reported to me, she invited me to join the meeting. I could feel the arctic chill in the air. That chill continued throughout our working relationship.

Initially, I thought I could fit in at Avon. I enjoyed the people I worked with, and I continued to grow in my marketing skills. I thought Avon was more in keeping with my assertive rather than aggressive personality. I was wrong. The people were more down to earth and less pretentious. They were like a family. That was a good thing. Even though my own family was loud and overbearing, I always knew they were there for me. We stuck together. My colleagues stuck together, as well. So much so that I found it difficult to crack the code and be accepted as part of the family. People would go around me and directly to my boss.

From my perspective, I did what I was hired to do. I made necessary changes. I brought fresh thinking to the business. The business grew under my leadership, and management was pleased. The eye portion of the business was up 68% and the total business was up 13%, when the rest of the industry was only up 1%. I proved myself and was excited. The time to receive my sign on bonus approached. I salivated at the thought of being rewarded for my hard work. During my prayer time, I sensed that Lord had other plans for my bonus. I thought, "I am definitely not hearing right. This cannot be from God." This was my money. I earned it. I waited so long for it. I was not ready to listen. I did not understand that it was not my money. This was one of those kicking and screaming moments. The Lord had to prepare my heart to give away my entire bonus. I had to learn to trust God with my finances. It took a month to get through the tantrum. I made a little progress. Even though I did not trust the Lord to provide for me, I did what I always did. I obeyed.

With all the successes on the business, I struggled. I was grateful that I had a team of assistants and associates to do all the analytical work for their respective businesses, but the company looked at financials and forecasts very differently than what I was used to in other companies. But certain things are basic. As an example, we were relaunching the lip and nail business. The manager who wanted to be promoted to Senior Manager developed the plans for the relaunch. When we met, I noticed that she did not forecast an increase in sales for either business even though we would be dedicating more resources in the coming year. I asked her to make changes. When we met with my boss the following day, it was evident that the manager did not make the changes. My boss called me out on it. I will never embarrass anyone, and I took the heat. It was downhill from there. It became painfully obvious to me that my subordinates were undermining me to management.

I was stressed. I worked around the clock. I arrived at work at 7:00 in the morning and left around 2:00 the next morning. I ran from meeting to meeting every day. I did not have time to think. I would plan out what I needed. When I finished one meeting, my assistant would take my files and hand me the information for the next meeting while I was on the run. I would get back to my office at the end of the day and try to deal with the day's workload. Without fail, management would drop major projects on us at 5:00 in the afternoon. They were always needed for the next morning. I delegated the workload to try and cover everything that needed to be done. I wondered if I made another mistake.

The unthinkable happened. It was a beautiful day on September 11, 2001. It was 9:00 in the morning, and I was chairing a meeting in the conference room. Suddenly, the door to the conference room swung open, and one of my associates came into the room. She was hysterical. I ran over to her and tried to get her to tell me what was wrong. Through her tears and hysteria, she spilled out that the planes had hit the World Trade Center. Her fiancé was in one of the towers. It took a moment to register what she just told me. I looked at everyone in the room and said, "This meeting is over!"

I grabbed my associate by the hand and brought her to my office. At this point, everyone scrambled to try to locate loved ones amid the chaos. Everything in the city was being shut down. We did our best to figure out what to do. In the frenzy, I ran into a coworker whose son was at school downtown. She was more concerned about a meeting and her presentation than trying to get to her son. I paused. It was as if I looked in a mirror. The cruel reality hit me that I always put work first. I felt a pang in my heart. But I could not focus on that. I needed to get back to my office to deal with my associate. She tried to contact her fiancé without any luck. I prayed the whole time and asked for wisdom. After a few hours, I suggested she call every message machine she could think of. It felt like an eternity. Finally, she called one machine, and her fiancé left a message for her. He said he made it out of the building and was alive. She broke down in my arms. We sat on the floor of my office. It was as if I escaped into my own little world the same as I did as a child. I shut everything out. Only this was not pretend. This was not a story I made up. This was real. It was just the two of us. I cradled her in my arms, and I stroked her hair. I needed to be strong for her. I needed to comfort her. Nothing else mattered. What mattered was she trusted me. What mattered was being human. She needed love. I gave it to her.

I looked out of the window onto Sixth Avenue. I saw people covered in ash. They looked like zombies as the shock was thick on their faces. I was numb. I could not cry. I just watched them make their way up Sixth Avenue. I asked, "Why, God. Why?" I turned around and there was a woman headed back to her desk. Our eyes connected. She just looked at me and started to cry. I went over to her and extended my arms. I just hugged her. There was nothing I could say or do but hug her. It was now 2:00 in the afternoon. I was not sure if I could get home. The city was locked down. There were no buses. There were no trains. Since I worked late hours, I drove into the city every day. I never got out of work in time to make the last train home. We were glued to the television set in the conference room. An announcement was made that the West Side Highway was open for traffic. I left the office. I retrieved my car and drove home with robotic precision.

I arrived home safely. I sat on my sofa. I was in shock. I did not cry. I did not feel. I just sat there. I needed to make sense of the horror. Again, I called out, "Why God, why?" I needed Him to answer. Nothing made any sense. I went to church that night. We prayed. We comforted each other. I reflected on the day and on my life. I could not let go of the split-second reality that hit me that day that I put work first. Would it take a tragedy like this to wake me up? Those people died without warning. I always said I did not want to go through life saying I should have. I knew work did not make me happy. What was my alternative? I headed to work the next day. I had to take the train since all the roads into the city were still closed. As I made my way through the parking lot, I looked up and saw my neighbor's car. He worked on Wall Street. I stood there and, in the middle of the parking lot, the magnitude of it all hit me. I broke down. It became so real. It became so personal. A stranger came over and comforted me. I pulled myself together and took the train into the city. At work, I could not stop thinking of my neighbor. When I got home that night, I noticed his car was not in the parking lot. I took a deep breath. When I got home, I saw him outside. I ran over to him. He was out of town on business. I believe it was a miracle. Another miracle that hit home for me was that my associate whose fiancé survived 9/11 asked the Lord Jesus Christ into her heart. I remember talking to my pastor's wife about this and how unhappy I was at work. She said that sometimes the Lord puts us on assignment. She said she believed I was placed at Avon for that moment with my associate.

I do not remember the days that followed. I was in a daze and on high alert at the same time. The air was thick with fear. The stress level was extremely high. My boss added more stress to my life. The week following 9/11, she told me that things were not working out. I knew they were not, but it felt like I was punched in the stomach. Again, what did I do wrong? She did not fire me. I needed to digest what she said. I could not think straight. I needed to figure out what to do. It just so happened that I had planned to take a cruise to Canada the following week. I was not sure if I should go or not. I decided to go. I needed to get away. I needed to process my life. I needed to seek God. Once on board, I settled into my cabin. It was just me and the Lord. I cried in prayer. I prayed each day. While away at sea and separated from everything and everyone, He answered me. I had come to know His voice. The Lord spoke to my heart while I was on my knees. It did not make any sense. I thought I was crazy.

Chapter 9
My Wake-Up Call

My business was soaring, and I was crashing. On 9/11, I witnessed life being snuffed out in a moment of horror and tragedy. I tried to wrap my head around what happened. I tried to make sense of the impact it had on me. That day added fear for my safety to the mix. I was in such a vulnerable place. I knew things were not working out. How many times do I have to go through the same thing? What was I missing?

I needed to get away. I needed divine guidance. I needed clear direction. While on the cruise to Canada, I was on my knees in prayer. Suddenly I heard that still small voice deep within utter one word to me. Just one word. The word was acting. Acting? Acting!?!   I thought I heard wrong. I needed wisdom. When the shipped docked, I found a phone. I called my sister, the one person with whom I could share anything. I never called her from vacation before. When she heard my voice, there was an immediate deep breath and a sound of concern in her voice. I told her I think the Lord spoke to me. I needed to know what she thought. She said, "What is it?" I hesitated. Then I said, "I heard one word. Acting." She did not say anything. "Sis, are you there?" She repeated, "Acting?" I told her I must have heard wrong. I asked, "What do you think?" In her infinite wisdom, she said, "Put it on the shelf. If this is God, it will happen."

One week later, I was back at work. Then, one morning in October 2001, I took my usual walk to work from the parking garage. This time was different. I walked very slowly. I did not want to go to work. I approached the building. I stopped. I wanted to scream. I leaned up against the building. I started to cry. I tried to pull myself together. I took a deep breath and forced myself to enter the building. I took the elevator to my floor and walked to my office. I put down my briefcase. I froze. I could not breathe. At that moment, a co-worker came into my office. She saw my distress and asked if I was alright. I started to hyperventilate. She immediately called 911. A small crowd started to form outside my office. People were concerned. I had such pain in my chest.

Fear gripped me. At the same time, it felt like everything went into slow motion. A coworker tried to keep me calm while waiting for the paramedics to arrive. It seemed like an eternity. When they arrived, they ordered people to get out of the way. After they checked me out, they put oxygen on my face and hoisted me onto a gurney. As they wheeled me out of the office, I could feel the eyes of every person bore into me. Fear was replaced with the concern of what they must be thinking of me. They must have thought I was weak. Even when I thought I was dying I was concerned about what people thought of me. How typical.

The nurse in the emergency room put nitroglycerine under my tongue as a precaution. I shook all over. I feared I was having a heart attack. Yet, I was concerned about all the work that needed to be done. How quickly I forgot about my reaction to the woman whose son was downtown on 9/11. My Senior Manager accompanied me to the hospital. She did her best to keep me calm while she tried to hide the incredulous look on her face. She assured me the work would get done. She told me I needed to focus on my health. She was right. My focus shifted to the sound of the heart monitor. Nothing but beep, beep, beep for hours. With every beep, the fear increased. I fought the emotion welling up inside of me. I tried to convince myself that everything would be all right. Finally, I was given good news. I suffered a panic attack.

All the stress, all the exhaustion, all the insanity finally caught up with me. What do I do now? Old habits die hard. I went back to work.

I needed to make a change. The Lord forced my hand. In November, I said to my assistant, "I wish I could just negotiate a package and get out of here. The next day, I received a call from Human Resources. The Director wanted to meet with me. I think the Holy Spirit prepared me for that meeting. A friend of mine at church worked in Human Resources at a major company. One day, I asked her to give me her perspective for a hypothetical situation. If I were to negotiate a severance package, what should be included. She thought for a moment, and she said, "At your level, it should be…"

As the Director and I talked, he said, "We realize you have not been happy here." His next words were like music. He said, "We'd like to offer you a severance package including a year's salary, full benefits, bonuses and stock options." Every word that he uttered mirrored what my friend told me. He then said, "what do you think? What did I think!?!

My assignment at Avon was finished. I danced out of the office that day. I was about start a new season in my life. But how? The answer came in the mail. I received a brochure from the Learning Annex in Manhattan. I saw there was a class on Commercials for Real People. It was as if in that moment I declared who I am. After years of wearing a façade, this real people emerged and wanted to do something different. The only connection I had to commercials was as the client. I worked behind the scenes to help develop the commercials, and I was instrumental in selecting the talent. This was the part of my job I enjoyed the most. I had a spark of excitement. I always wanted to be in front of the camera. After a 22-year marketing career that did not seem possible.

I had no preconceived notions about the class. I was lighthearted and felt no pressure. I just wanted to have some fun. When I arrived, it was obvious I was the oldest person in the class. I was surrounded by teeny boppers chomping at the bit to be discovered. I took a seat and waited for the class to begin. The teacher came into the room and introduced himself. He was a manager of some renown in the industry and in New York City. This was my opportunity to get information, and I was not shy about asking questions. I found the evening well worth my time. I thanked the teacher and was appreciative of him sharing his insights with the class. I intended to just file that information away. I received a surprise the following day. He contacted me. He said he was impressed with my professionalism. He recommended I start taking some commercial acting classes, and he gave me a referral. Being a businesswoman, I thought this was a scam. I did some homework, and I discovered it was legitimate. I signed up to take commercial classes. I drove down twice a week into the city. I had a blast. I had no stress. I was just having fun. Then, one thing led to another. I was introduced to a teacher who taught acting for TV and film. We hit it off, and I started taking classes from him. I also started studying voiceover. I drove into the city three to four times a week. I was not sure what I was doing, but I was a sponge. I absorbed everything. I started to meet people and I was introduced to a manager in the city. I started to intern for her; and without realizing it, she had me audition for a voiceover commercial. She asked me to speak to a director on the phone. He liked the sound of my voice, and I booked a local commercial.

As I networked, I was introduced to a wonderful casting director who also worked for a theatre company in the city. She had many contacts in the industry, and she produced a showcase every year to present new talent to agents and managers. My confidence was building, and I decided to participate. I worked for several weeks on a scene with a scene partner. I think all those years of being in front of management and doing presentations helped me stay calm. I was not at all nervous. The next day I received a call from an agent who attended the showcase. He said he loved my performance and wanted to meet with me. I kept my cool and set up an appointment with him. We immediately hit it off and he signed me up as a client. Within a week, he set me up on my first major television audition. It was for Law & Order. The role was for a government clerk, and I was well prepared. There were several interruptions during the audition. The casting associate had children, and her nanny was sick. She was trying to find an alternate sitter for her kids.

I told her I understood. I mentioned that I taught Sunday School and I learned that, with kids, anything can happen. She smiled and chatted for a little bit. She thanked me and I left.

The next day, my agent called me. He said I had a callback for a Producer/Director session. He said, they wanted me to audition for the role of the Jury Foreperson. He said that it was not unusual to change a role. I had my audition date and time. Again, I was prepared. The day of my audition I had an appointment with my gynecologist. I had plenty of time between my doctor's appointment and the audition. As I sat in the examining room and wore nothing but a paper robe, my agent called. He wanted to explain to me that a Producer/Director session was a big deal but not to be nervous. I thought, "If you only knew where I was, you would know that the audition is nothing in comparison." He told me that there would be several producers in the room, most likely including Dick Wolf. I just said, "Okay, I appreciate you letting me know." I was such a newbie at acting it was a blessing that I did not have a clue that it was a big deal.

I arrived at the Chelsea Piers on the west side of Manhattan for my audition. I wanted to learn and take in the whole experience. I just went with the flow. I was ushered into the room for my audition. To my surprise, it was packed with producers, writers, the director, and casting. I had two scenes prepared, as there were two jury foremen in this episode. The first scene found the defendant not guilty. The second scene found the same defendant guilty. I did my first read. Then I did the second read. One of the producers said, "Can't you make up your mind." I tend to have a quick wit and I did not get flustered. I just looked at him and said, "It's such a big decision." They laughed. That was it.

I returned to my car and started to second guess my comment to the producer. I called my agent to let him know about the audition. I told him what transpired between me and the producer, and I was concerned that maybe I should not have said anything. He told me not to worry. They love that kind of thing. Okay. The next day my agent called and said, "You're Jury Foreman #1". I said, "I don't understand." He said, "YOU BOOKED THE ROLE!" The only thing I remember is that, at first, there was dead silence and then I screamed. I booked my very first role for a MAJOR TV show. Then, it got even better. My agent told me I was going to get paid. I said, "I get paid too." He just laughed.

The day arrived, and I showed up at the studio for my first acting gig. I signed in and was escorted to my dressing room. It was smaller than a tiny closet and located in the main room where the extras congregated. I did not care. I called my sister and told her I was calling from my dressing room. I was beside myself happy. I was then ushered to hair and makeup. In the next chair was Sam Waterston. I remained calm and professional. I so wanted to say hello, but I knew not to. I needed to go to the rest room, and behind me was Jerry Orbach. He actually talked to me. He was so friendly and funny. I was then called to the set. I was on the set of Law & Order. Someone had to pinch me. I heard right when I heard the Lord drop the word acting into my spirit. God took my dream off the shelf. I was now living my dream. I took my place in the jury box. We rehearsed. During rehearsal, I made a newbie mistake. I neglected to stand when I read out the verdict. Sam Waterston called it out. I got a twinge in the pit of my stomach. But that was it. It was just a twinge. I did not let it get to me. Was it because I was living my dream, and nothing was going to take it away from me? We rehearsed the scene again, and it was perfect. We shot the scenes. They went off without a hitch. I was on cloud nine. The icing on the cake was that I qualified to get my SAG card first shot out of the barrel. People try for years to get that revered union card. I thought this is easy. I think the Lord dangled a carrot in front of me so I would pursue my childhood dream.

Auditions were few and far between. Time ticked along, and I started to think I need to get work. I immediately fell back into the corporate mindset. I interviewed with a small, sports equipment company for the position of Vice President. Vice President was the elusive title I strived to achieve for years. Now it was right before me. I headed into the city for my fourth interview with the company. The fourth time opened my eyes. A young woman sat across from me on the train. She had two briefcases with her. She frantically moved from one bag to the other as she worked on a presentation. She looked so stressed out. Like a thunderbolt, it hit me. I cannot do this anymore.

I needed to earn money. In the words of my mother, "Acting does not put food on the table." Acting may not have put food on the table, but it fed my soul. As for earning money, I decided to put my business skills to use and partnered with a consulting company. I became an independent consultant that afforded me the opportunity to earn a living and the freedom to pursue my passion. This made sense to me. I needed things to make sense. But I knew deep inside that I should not do it. The Lord confirmed that consulting was not the road I should take. Out of the forty-five appointments made for me, I broke the record for no shows and cancelled appointments. I had one long-term client. She ran the family business. When we first met, I listened intently for two hours. My immediate response was, "You need to be validated." It was as if I said it to myself. She wanted to sign a contract to meet with me every day. Even though I needed money, I would not violate my ethics. I realized she was vulnerable, and I would not take advantage of her. I made a recommendation and followed up with her. I followed up for a few months without any results. I began to wonder if I should have closed on a contract of some kind the day we met. I, then, got a flash thought that she did not need a consultant. She needed a mentor. I reached out to her with my new proposal. She answered within in minutes. I met with her once a week. We formed a solid business relationship which blossomed into a long friendship. Her family adopted me, and I adopted them. She opened my eyes that it is not about work. It is about relationship. It is about trust.

I believe our meeting was a divine appointment. I helped her and she encouraged me in my pursuit of acting. As good a relationship as this was, I could not earn a living off one client. I knew I was not on the right path with the business. On February 26, 2003, I closed in with the Lord and prayed for direction. It was then I sensed the Lord tell me that I would move to Los Angeles. I did not want to move to Los Angeles. I did not like Los Angeles. I often flew to Los Angeles to film commercials, and I could not wait to get home. After I had one of my tantrums, I asked the Lord to forgive me. I asked Him to make it clear when the move would happen.

The business was not working, and I still pursued acting. I was again in prayer when I sensed, "Sell your house now." "Where am I going?" "Los Angeles." I hoped the Lord changed His mind. This was big. I needed spiritual guidance. I made an appointment with my pastors. I brought my journal with me. I showed then my entry when I sensed the Lord would move me to LA. I will never forget what my pastor said. "God would not move you to LA." I now faced a big test. Would I trust that I heard from God, or would I listen to an authority figure who knew more than I did spiritually? I was confused. I was fearful. I once again cried out for direction. The Lord led me to Genesis Chapter 12:1(NIV) "The Lord said to Abram, 'Go from your country, your people and your father's household to the land I will show you." I took a deep breath. I knew moving to Los Angeles was the right decision.

I called a friend of mine who was a real estate agent. She came over and we developed a plan to put my home on the market. At the time, it was a seller's market. I decided to test the waters and I took a trip to Los Angeles. I got the lay of the land, and I performed in front of agents, managers, and casting directors. I also took advantage of an offer from a casting director I met at a workshop in New York. She liked my work and said, "If you're ever in Los Angeles, stop by." Well, I did. I drove across town to the CBS lot and drove up to the gate. Again, it was pouring. When I got to the gate, a very burly security guard approached my car. I told him why I was there. He asked if I had an appointment. I did not. He said he could not let me in, but he also said I was at the wrong gate. I apologized and asked what is the right gate? I found the other gate entrance and was met by a more approachable security guard. I told him why I was there and who I would like to see. I told him what she had said at the workshop in New York. He told me to wait while he called her. To my surprise, he said she would see me. I was delighted and stunned at the same time. We met for 15 minutes. When we finished, she said, "I admire your persistence. Most people would have given up after they were turned away from the first gate." I thought, "I just flew 3,000 miles from New York to Los Angeles and drove across town in the pouring rain. I am not going to give up that easily. Yep, I am persistent."

It was a long and busy week. I met some wonderful people, learned some key insights about living and working in Los Angeles. When I returned to New York, two agents called me. They were interested in representing me. I explained that I was still in New York and was preparing to move to Los Angeles at the beginning of the year. I kept in touch with them.

In November, I received an offer on my home. It fell through. Another offer. It too fell through. I started to wonder if I heard correctly. It was a Wednesday evening, and as I sat on my sofa, I asked the Lord to confirm that I was to move to Los Angeles. On Sunday, I had two offers on my home. There was a bidding war. I learned a few things from the offers that fell through. I wanted to make sure that the potential buyers were financially sound. I decided to go with the lower offer. The family was being relocated by the husband's company, and they could put down 50% of the asking price. I miraculously signed a contract by Christmas, and I was on a plane January 2, 2005 to fly to Los Angeles to look for a place to live.

There were torrential downpours for the entire week I searched for a place to live. I quickly learned that when it rains in LA, people do not show up for appointments. It is as if they will melt in the rain.

I showed up to look at apartments and no one would be available to show me the property. When I did see apartments within my budget, I felt they needed to be torched. I was wet and discouraged. I called my sister. We talked through my experiences. She wisely suggested that I needed to up my budget. She knew I would be miserable if my housing was unsuitable. I ventured out again. My windshield wipers could not go fast enough. The rain was so heavy I could not see in front of me. I pulled off to the side of the road. I asked the Lord for help. Again, that still small voice within whispered, "Go to the next light and make a left." I did. Within two blocks, I saw an apartment complex with a sign out front that said, 'newly renovated.' I decided to park my car and check it out. The manager was in her office and miraculously the rain stopped. She showed me two apartments. I was blown away. They were gorgeous and large. It was a relief that all my furniture would fit. I was down to the wire. My luggage was in the car as I met with the manager to sign my lease. I called my attorney and requested that he send a copy of the contract on the sale of my home to the manager to prove that I was financially sound. The contract came through. I signed the lease and headed to the airport. Everything fell into place.

I was scheduled to move to Los Angeles on February 11th. The movers came on February 5th. I knew it would take a week for the movers to make it across the country with my belongings. I was a gypsy for a week as I planned to make the rounds to say goodbye to everyone. There was a blizzard every week that winter, and the day the moving van came was no exception. At 7:00 a.m., I looked out of my window and the snow was coming down heavy. Another miracle happened. The moving van arrived at 8:00 a.m. It was like the parting of the Red Sea. The snow stopped and the sun came out. I knew it was a sign. The movers were able to get everything done in the allotted amount of time. They no sooner loaded the last piece of furniture the clouds formed, and the snow started again.

It was now time to say goodbye to my church family. There was a tradition at the church when people moved on. The elders would call the person up front, and the elders and pastors would circle around them, pray over them, and send them off with a blessing. That did not happen with me. The pastor announced I was moving to Los Angeles and asked people to extend their hands toward me and pray for me. The elders did not circle around me, nor did they pray a blessing over me. It took quite a while to say goodbye to everyone, but I felt short changed that the leadership did not pray or bless me. I took offense. I left for Los Angeles and carried this offense with me. I learned from scripture that if we are offended by a brother or sister in the Lord, we should go to them. I wrote a letter to the pastor. He called me and was livid. He said I was rebellious and needed to get right with the Lord. I never considered myself rebellious. I was obedient. Looking back, I was rebellious. I rebelled against an authority figure in my life. I knew I was right with God. I was no longer a young Christian. I had grown. I prayed. I sought His direction. I was respectful enough to seek godly counsel. I rejected it. I respected myself. I obeyed the sound of the Lord's voice. He is my ultimate authority. I stepped out in faith. I started to trust the Lord. I left the past behind. My pastor and I never spoke again.

Chapter 10
A Step of Faith

I moved to California on my terms. I left everything and everyone behind to follow my passion. It was a big risk, and I did not have a safety net. I did not know a soul. To the logical mind, this was nuts. I am not some young spring chicken. I am a mature woman, and I moved to a place that idolizes youth and beauty. The odds are against me. This was huge for someone who is always responsible and follows the straight and narrow path. It defied logic, and I defied my pastors. Even so, I had peace and it felt right. My parents were not crazy about the idea, but they understood; or should I say, my father understood my need to do it. This was a new phase in my life. I would soon learn that my journey included many ups and downs, twists and turns, joys and disappointments but, mostly, a deeper walk with the Lord and learning to trust Him.

When I flew to Los Angeles in October to get the lay of the land, I received many insights on making the move. One of the insights I received was to fly into Long Beach and not LAX. It was less overwhelming and easier to get around. That is what I did. When I arrived in Long Beach, the monsoons continued. I found my way to my rental car. I was soaked and miserable. I now had about an hour drive to Los Angeles. My apartment would not be available until Monday, and it was Friday night. I arranged to stay at the Marriott Courtyard using my hotel points. It felt like an eternity to drive to the hotel. The rain was so heavy that I could not see in front of me. Again, the windshield wipers could not go fast enough. I remember thinking, "If rain means blessings from God, I'm in for an avalanche." I drove at a snail's pace, and it took two hours to drive to the hotel. I finally arrived and could not get to my room fast enough. I was exhausted and wanted to get out of my wet clothes, take a shower and go to bed.

The next day, my type A personality was in full throttle. I woke up early because I had scheduled a workshop at 9:00 in the morning. Who arrives in town at midnight and goes to class the next morning? Me! The instructor asked, "Who is the newest arrival in Los Angeles." I won hands down. At that workshop, I discovered something about myself. In class, the consensus was that I was a comedian. This surprised me. I saw myself as a dramatic actress. All those years in corporate did not allow me to see myself as I truly am. I am funny. I never registered that people laugh when I am around them.

They laugh with me not at me. As a new believer, I sensed the Lord tell me through a song that He saw me as laughter. The laughter I received during my scene reinforced this truth about myself. That day, I stepped into my destiny to release the fountain of joy within me.

After class, I decided to go to the apartment complex and make sure that everything was going according to schedule. When I did a walkthrough of my apartment, I noticed that they did not replace the carpet. I brought this to the manager's attention. I may have discovered my inner joy that morning, but the businesswoman was also alive and well. I have a keen eye and an attention for detail. The manager was not happy. They needed to scurry to replace the carpet for my Monday move-in date. I drove around trying to acquaint myself with my new neighborhood. On Sunday morning, I went to the only church I was familiar with from watching Christian TV in New York. I picked up some brochures after the service and noticed they had a bible study on the Song of Songs. I had just finished a year-long bible study in New York on the Song of Songs. It was wonderful. I thought I would get another perspective and add to what I had already learned. Having a church family and studying the bible are important to me. It grounded me.

I soon learned that God dangled a carrot in front of me to get me to move to Los Angeles. Things would not be easy on many fronts. On Monday, I called the two agents who showed interest in me back in October. I let them know that I moved. It took several weeks to get appointments to meet with them. When I finally did meet with them, one of the agents soon went out of business and the other decided not to pursue a relationship with me. I was now new in town with no agent or prospects. I had a plan.

A friend of mine in New York had a dear friend in Los Angeles who was a commercial casting director. I called her and we chatted for a while. I decided to take her commercial acting class and she referred me to a theatrical acting teacher located in Venice, CA. I had no idea how far Venice was from where I lived. But a recommendation is a recommendation. In New York, I studied the Meisner Acting Technique and was used to a more organic approach. I was now introduced to Method Acting. I felt a tugging not to study with her. I rationalized that she came highly recommended and stick with it. I could not find my footing. For me, it was too analytical. It reminded me of crunching numbers back in my marketing days. I hated it. I realized I tried to force fit myself into something that was not right for me. I just took the biggest risk of my life so I could be free to be me. I should have listened to my inner voice that screamed this is not for you.

That message became very clear. One day, I arrived early to class. She was coaching a young actress of about 18 years old for an audition. I was stunned. The teacher screamed at this young actress to get her to the next level for her audition. I believe it is important to treat people with respect. I never treated my subordinates the way she treated that student. I did not treat my students in Sunday School that way, and they were kids. I was incensed that she would talk to a student like that. How dare she humiliate this actress in front of others? I did not say anything, but I made a mental note. I struggled as I studied with this teacher for a month. I decided to call her to discuss things with her. She bluntly told me, "If you can't do this, then you are not an actress." I shocked myself with my response. I simply said, "You are no longer my teacher." I had gained respect for myself, and I would not allow anyone to disrespect me or my efforts. I must admit it felt good. I was not angry when I said it. I was calm. I was direct. I moved on. I was proud of myself.

I participated in acting workshops, and I decided to jump into a weekend event that enabled me to perform in front of many casting directors, agents, and managers. I did my thing and was even nominated for best performance of a dramatic monologue. I received some high praise for my work, but I was the mother of the group. I was surrounded by teeny boppers. The focus was on them. I did meet an agent and she gave me her card. I contacted her the following week, and I quickly received an appointment to meet with the owner of the agency. We hit it off. I was so excited. I was with the agency three months when the owner announced he was closing his doors. He made the decision to pursue his acting career. I spoke with the agent who introduced me to him, and she explained that she was blindsided. She had no idea he was planning to close the agency. My excitement crashed and burned. I was back to square one.

I felt Hollywood had some code I needed to crack, and I did not have the key. It would take patience and persistence. The same held true for figuring out how to get around the city. Los Angeles is so spread out and it takes forever to get anywhere. I thought New York traffic was bad. I never thought I would say that I missed the New York subway and the buses. The freeways can be scary and confusing. I needed to take the 405 freeway. After driving for a while, I realized I should have been there by now. I was not on the 405. I was on the 101. It took forever to backtrack to get where I was going. The joke about the 405 freeway is that it takes about four to five hours to get anywhere. I feel that is a metaphor for Hollywood. Would I ever get to where I am going in my career? I seem to have the green light to go down one road and then I come to a screeching halt.

On the church front, things also were not what I thought they would be. I called the minister who was going to teach the bible study on the Song of Songs. We started talking. He said, "You sound like one of those hungry ones." He then told me about a church in Pasadena that was scheduled to hold a conference on The Father's Heart. I said, "I'm still trying to figure out where the grocery store is. Where's Pasadena?" He said he thought I would enjoy the conference. I was surprised that he suggested I attend a different church. I could not shake my pastor in New York who often said, "You don't need to go to other churches or listen to other people to hear the word of God." I was conflicted, but I thought about it and went on the church's website. It was the last day to register for the conference. I decided to attend. I was blown away by, not only the speakers, but by the praise and worship. I was on my knees and tears streamed down my face. I was also overwhelmed by the majesty of the Ambassador Auditorium. It was so grand with gold leaf on the ceiling panels, winding staircases, crystal chandeliers and a ladies' room that had marble flooring and more than two stalls. I could not stop looking around. It is so opulent. I felt uncomfortable. I was used to small churches with no frills. I wondered if God was this grand.

I could not stop thinking about that church and the conference, but I felt that the Lord had shown me the first church. I thought that is where I am to go. I look back now and laugh at how rigid I was. I could not open myself up to think that the Lord used the first church to guide me to Harvest Rock in Pasadena. One Sunday morning, I had the grand plan of attending the 8:30 a.m. service at Harvest Rock and then attend the 11:00 a.m. service at the first church. A miracle happened that morning. I sat in the back of the auditorium when the Senior Pastor walked up the aisle. He saw me and came over. He introduced himself and said, "I have not seen you here before." I told him it was my first time at the service. He welcomed me. Then, another man came up the aisle and came over to me. He introduced himself to me. As we chatted, he told me he was also from New York. He invited me to sit with him and his wife. I agreed. After the praise and worship, his wife leaned over and asked me, "What are you doing after church," I felt foolish telling her I was going to go to the other church. I just said, "Why do you ask?" I almost fell out of my chair. She invited me to join them for breakfast after the service. That touched me because, as a newbie in any other church, I was never invited to join anyone after the service for a get together. During breakfast, we chatted and got to know each other. Then, they paid for my breakfast. I just looked at them. I wondered could they be this nice. All they wanted to do was bless me. That morning I saw and received Christian love in action. I cannot explain why, but this made me uncomfortable.

It took four months for me to get the message to move over to Harvest Rock. One Sunday morning, tears streamed down my face as I worshiped. A deacon came over and asked if I was okay. It hit me that if you cannot tell that I am deep in worship, then something is very wrong here. I knew I was to move on. I had a peace about my decision. It felt right. I started to listen more carefully to the voice deep within me. Harvest Rock became my new church home and I quickly got involved. I volunteered to teach Sunday School. I also decided to join the home group of the couple who invited me to breakfast. I made friends and it felt like I had family. I was also introduced to an actress who was part of the group. She too was from New York, and we hit it off. I quickly realized there are Christians in Hollywood. I was not alone. My career and spiritual life began to merge. My new friend invited me to join her to attend a rehearsal for the show The Drowsy Chaperone. She had a friend in the cast, and the play was scheduled to open at the Ahmanson Theatre before going to Broadway. The rehearsal hall was such an intimate setting. Folding chairs were set up for those invited to watch the rehearsal. I looked around and noticed that I sat amongst some recognizable actors and actresses in the industry. I knew to play it cool and not appear star struck.

The rehearsal started, and I had a blast. I laughed so hard that I snorted, and my stomach hurt. I was embarrassed and delighted at the same time. I almost fell out of my folding chair I laughed so hard. After the rehearsal, we hung out to wait for my friend's friend. While we waited, the two lead actors saw me and came over. They told me how much I thrilled them with my reaction to the show and they loved my infectious laughter. My once hearty, unprofessional laugh was now accepted and appreciated by my peers. This opened the door for me to accept the fact that my laugh reflects the real me. It is my gift that sets me apart, so much so, that I added it to my acting resume as a special skill. Jokingly, the lead actor said, "Can we pay you to come to the show?" I was tickled and surprised. My delight continued. I was introduced to the director. I told him how much I enjoyed the show. I told him that I had seen so many Broadway shows, and this was a definite hit. I was even so bold and moved to say that the show would win at least five Tony awards. It did. My friend's friend finally joined us, and I was introduced to her. Then, to my surprise she invited us to opening night and the after party at the Dorothy Chandler Pavilion. I was in heaven. I wore my best evening attire. I took my seat and settled in for the evening. The grandeur of the Ahmanson Theater and the full staging and costumes made it feel like I was seeing the show for the first time. My laughter reverberated through the entire theatre. I was so excited to be there. I always wanted to go to an opening night. It was a dream come true. Next was the after party. I did not know what to expect. I was at an event with A list celebrities who all hob knobbed with each other. I was on the outside looking in. I thought, "One day they will be hob knobbing with me."

I just knew the show would win five Tony Awards. As I became more aware of my prophetic gifting, I attended a class at the church entitled, The School of the Prophets. I needed to understand more about the gift within me. When I attended the first class, I was a stranger to mostly everyone there. The teachers, David and Jeanie Richardson arrived. As Jeanie made her way down the aisle, she came over to me and introduced herself. Then she said, "I'd like to talk with you after class." I started shaking. My brain immediately went to that dark place that I was in trouble. Anytime a teacher told me they wanted to see me after class it meant I did something wrong, and I was going to be punished. Logically, that did not make any sense. I never met Jeanie before that moment. I could not focus on the class. All I could think about was the fact that Jeanie wanted to see me.

Class was over, and I made my way up to the front. Jeanie was engaged in conversation with other students, and I waited patiently. I was trained from childhood never to interrupt another person. When I was in elementary school and sent on an errand to another classroom, I had to knock on the door and wait for someone to acknowledge me. I could never just open the door, walk in, and deliver the message. That sense of protocol has stayed with me to this day.

When Jeanie turned and acknowledged me, I gulped. We chatted for a moment and then she shocked me. She said, "You have such a prophetic anointing. I would like you to pray about being part of a prophetic prayer team for the upcoming Prophetic Conference in January." I needed to digest what she said. How did she know I had a prophetic anointing? I immediately wanted to say NO WAY! I paused and I told her I would pray about it. I did, and I felt I was to join one of the teams. I was so nervous about it. Thankfully, the conference was in January, and this was October. I was able to take a few classes to get a better understanding of the prophetic, before I ventured out at the conference. The day finally arrived. What if I hear wrong? What if I do not get anything for anyone? What if…??? The team leader and the team members could not have been more cordial and loving. The leader laid out the rules for the team. God really showed up, and He enabled me to bless individuals who needed to hear from God. My journey to grow in my gifting had officially started. I felt I could not be in a better place under better tutelage.

After a year of teaching Sunday school, I sensed I was to volunteer for the Ministry Team. David and Jeanie were the Directors. I filed an application, and I was accepted. There was a caveat. Jeanie told me that I needed to wait for six months before I could participate. I did not understand why. It then became obvious. She saw some things in me that needed to be healed before I could minister to others. I so wanted to live the abundant life Jesus promised, I would do whatever was necessary to get there. I have learned to recognize when the Lord wants to deal with me. Another layer of rejection had to be healed. It was painful, but my tenacity to fight moves me forward and enables me to let God do whatever He has to do to heal me body, soul, and spirit. The Lord freed me up, and I was welcomed onto the Ministry Team.

That was not the end. The Lord wanted to deal with me again. I needed to be healed of my fear of authority. After a Sunday service, I got that nudge from the Holy Spirit that I knew all too well. He nudged me to go up to Pastor Che Ahn and ask him to pray for me to be delivered from the fear of authority. I freaked out. He was authority. I could not do it. I dug in my heels. It was as if the Holy Spirit grabbed me by the collar and personally brought me to the front of the sanctuary. I waited my turn to speak with pastor. I could not even look him in the eyes. My head was down, and I spoke so fast. I said, "Pastor, the Holy Spirit dragged me up here to be delivered from the fear of authority." Pastor Che impressed me as someone who had no fear. He said, "Well, that has to go." He then put his hand on my head and commanded the fear of authority to leave me. With my head still lowered, I turned to leave and BOOM! I fell down under the power of the Holy Spirit. I was shaking for about a half an hour. I finally was able to get up, and I felt lighter. From that day forward, authority figures did not have the same hold over me. I would be tested. With each test, I needed to decide if I would bow to man or to God.

I pursued the Lord and grew as a Christian. I became more confident in my spiritual gifting and was, eventually, moved from prayer ministry to prophetic ministry which promoted me to leading a team at the annual prophetic conference. My growth in the prophetic was instrumental not only in church but in being able to navigate Hollywood. I was on two paths. Church opened up the spiritual realm which prepared me to deal with Hollywood, its competitive bent and all the rejection that goes with it. I needed to be strengthened to pursue my life-long dream. Neither path was quite what I expected.

I did not know what to expect in Hollywood. I innocently thought that, since I followed the Lord's leading, things would happen quickly. For almost three years, I put one foot in front of the other. I tried to figure out the industry and how to break in. There was a flicker of light. I met the casting director for General Hospital, and she offered me a role as a background player for one episode of the show. She explained that she liked to see how professional an actor is before she considered them for a speaking role. I was grateful. I did the role and, not too soon, after that, I was offered a speaking role on the spinoff show, General Hospital Night Shift. Then, I was given a voice over role for the main show, General Hospital. Things were starting to happen for me. I booked those roles with no representation. I was, then, introduced to a manager. We hit it off, and she took me on as a client. Soon after signing on, I auditioned for and booked a role in the feature film, He's Just Not That into You. I was thrilled. I arrived on set and met the most amazing people. I asked questions and gleaned so much as I watched the director interact with the actors and crew. I was on set from early in the morning until I was called at about 6:00 pm. I was the consummate professional. We did two rehearsals and then shot the scene. After the day's events, I was notified by my manager that the director wanted my information sent to him for his files. I have kept in touch with him to this day. I was on my way.

The bottom fell out. The Writer's Strike hit in 2007, the industry was shut down for months and things were looking very bleak. Things went from bad to worse. The stock market crashed in 2008 and fear gripped, not only the industry, but the country. I had a vision of the buildings in the financial district in New York being bounced around like rubber bands. I did not know that vision was prophetic. I had been given a warning. I did not understand it, and I did not take my investments out of the market. I lost half of my savings. The savings

I used to live on while I pursued my dream. My dream became a nightmare. I was scared. I was not sure what to do next.

Chapter 11
Moving Forward

2008 started out with a bright spot for me, despite the financial crisis and the writer's strike. The film, He's Just Not That into You, was released in February that year. I went to one of the screenings on the studio lot. I dressed up for the event. I should have dressed for the weather. There was another downpour. I felt and looked like drowned rat. I did not care. I was about to experience what I always wanted. I was about to see myself on the big screen. It was surreal. I did not know when I appeared in the film. To my delight, my scene was placed in the first ten minutes of the film. When I saw myself, I gasped and put my hands over my mouth. I did not want to draw attention to myself. I took it in. I knew I belonged.

I did not have the experience of walking the red carpet at the screening. It did not matter. The week the filmed opened, I was invited to a friend's home after Sunday service. When I arrived, my friends started blowing horns and releasing confetti. I was stunned and gleefully surprised. They placed a bouquet of flowers in my arms and escorted me down the red carpet they placed at the door and into the living room. It was their way of congratulating me on my film debut. I was given a small Oscar statue to commemorate the event. I laughed and cried at the same time. My church family blessed my socks off. I was so touched. I felt so special.

My wonderful film debut experience was short lived. I needed to face the reality that I could not seem to get any acting work. I applied for jobs that some would be considered survival jobs for an actor, but nothing materialized. My resources were more limited than before, and I started to panic about money. How was I going to live? I did everything I knew to do. I put one foot in front of the other and moved forward. I focused on the business side of acting. I needed to network. I joined an organization called the Actor's Network which was established to educate actors on the business side of acting. I understood business, but I still needed to get a grasp on Hollywood and the industry. I attended seminars and industry guest events. Walking away from corporate was not easy, but corporate was very much a part of me. Connecting and being accountable is ingrained in me. Only now I work for myself. Through the organization, I joined a group that met once a month. I set goals for myself and shared them with the group. I then shared my progress on achieving those goals. I was offered objective suggestions and insights from others. This kept my juices pumping and kept me on track. I was in my comfort zone, and I was being proactive and responsible.

It is through the Actor's Network that I met two amazing teachers that would have an impact on my life. I studied with a husband-and-wife team for two years. They encouraged me and helped me grow as an actress. They were like family, but I felt I plateaued. I listened to my inner voice and started to explore working with other teachers. I could not allow myself to get complacent. The first teacher I met helped me learn how to breathe properly and how-to bring power to my voice. He was also a writer, and I studied with him to bring out the stories that were within me. I found his technique interesting. I had never studied writing before. Being an actress, I first acted out my stories and then wrote them down. I expressed myself and brought life to my stories. I put my toe in the water and started to develop as a writer. I discovered my voice. I discovered I had a story to tell. I needed the courage to step out and tell it my way.

As I learned to write, I felt I needed to grow as an actress. I signed up for a special Class at the Actor's Network, where I met award winning actor and director, Philip Charles MacKenzie. He was at a place in his career where he wanted to teach. During the class he asked volunteers to participate in an acting exercise. I volunteered. I took to it like a duck takes to water. I enjoyed working with Philip that day. Only, I did not start to study with him right away. I waited until I felt it was time to move on. I believe it is one of the best decisions I ever made in pursuing my acting career. He treated me with respect and saw my potential. He was open and honest and pushed me to be better. I remember one of the first scenes I ever did in his class. I pulled out Martha from Who's Afraid of Virginia Wolf. Even though I received rave reviews for my audition from the director of the community theater in Connecticut, I felt I needed to master this character. After I finished my scene, Philip started asking me relevant questions. My takeaway was that I was terrible, and I made so many mistakes. I broke down and started to cry. After class, he called me over said that he would like to take some time and talk with me outside of class. We arranged for a telephone call. Something amazing happened on that call. Once he got to know me a bit better, he recognized that I was still very corporate, and I was afraid to let go of myself and become the character. In the corporate world, I stuffed my emotions. I grew up in the era of never let them see you sweat. I carried that into my acting. The corporate wall I built needed to come down. Little by little, I began to understand about living in the moment. I consider Philip a blessing in my life. He never let me settle. He knew what I had in me. I trusted him. I studied with him for 12 years. I believe I will study with him again.

I wanted to continue to study, but money was tight. I was pinching pennies and tried to be very frugal. I have always been someone who lived within my means. If I could not afford it, I did not buy it. I looked for alternate ways to work my acting muscles. I felt frustrated and wondered if things would ever turn around. Suddenly, I was hit with a body blow. One Sunday, I was at church, and I was very agitated. I did not understand why. My family tried to reach me, but I was outside of the range for my cellphone. When I returned home, I listened to the messages and learned that my mother had a massive stroke and was airlifted to a major medical facility for care. At church, the Holy Spirit gave me a warning. He prepared me. I knew when I heard the news that this was it. I spoke to her the day before, and she told me she was not feeling well. That was not like her. She would always put on that everything is fine persona. She did not want me to worry. All I could think about was that my last words to my mother were, "I love you, Mom."

I quickly arranged to fly to New Jersey the following day. On the flight back east, I started writing my mother's eulogy. Before I left, I asked my father to keep her on life support until I arrived. I wanted closure. Several years before, one of my dear friends died suddenly from a mitral valve prolapse that went undetected. She was 47 years old and seemed to be the picture of health. I had sensed to call her, but I kept putting it off, and then I could not call her. Her husband left me a message that she had passed away. I was so broken. I felt so guilty that I did not listen to that still small voice within me. I did not want to go through that again. My father thought I was going to fight the DNR, but that was not the case at all. Even though my mother was on life support; she was still technically alive. My cousins picked me up at Newark Airport and drove me to the hospital. I kept it together. I think that was mostly for my father. I knew she was going to be in heaven, and I would see her again.

That assurance came early one Sunday morning. I sensed I was to call my mother and ask her to forgive me for witnessing to her about Jesus for 17 years. I sensed she was offended that I did not respect her Catholic faith. I called her early and asked her to forgive me. My mother being my mother said, "You don't have to do that." I said, "Yes I do, Mom." We chatted, and I explained that I just wanted to her to understand who Jesus is regarding her faith. I told her that I had asked Jesus into my heart, and I knew that was the right thing to do. There was a long pause. My mother asked me, "How did you do that?" "Do what, Mom?" "How did you ask Jesus into your heart?" I told her I said what is called the sinner's prayer. Again, there was a pause. Then, "Can I say that prayer." "Of course, Mom." It took an act of obedience and humility on my part to experience one of the most tender moments with my mother. My love for her poured out through every fiber of my being. Tenderly, I assured her that when her time came, she would be in heaven. She received the greatest gift of all four days before her 82nd birthday.

When I arrived at the hospital, my family surrounded my mother's bedside. They knew to leave the room and give me some private time with her. My cousin, Mark, stayed in the room with me and stood at the foot of the bed. I stroked my mother's arm and held her hand. I then said, for the last time, "I love you, Mom." When I said that phrase that she needed to hear so many times before, her foot jerked. My cousin looked at me and said, "Did you see that?" I filled up with tears and said, "She heard me." It was then I knew it was time to say goodbye. I left the room. I saw my family at the door. I thanked my father for keeping her on life support until I arrived and had some time with her. We formed a small circle, held hands, and prayed. Once the life support was removed, my sister and I went back into the room. I started to shake. I sensed the presence of angels as they escorted my mother's spirit to heaven. She died at Thanksgiving 2009. We had the wake on Wednesday, a small Thanksgiving on Thursday, and the funeral on Friday. I delivered the eulogy. My family was so moved as I shared heartfelt stories about my mom. We were opposites, and she did not understand me or I her, but we loved each other.

Before I left for New Jersey, I was introduced to a manager. We met when I returned to Los Angeles. We had a great conversation and decided to work together. Within a week, she set up an audition for me on the new TV show, Parenthood. I was grateful for the audition, but I was still caught up in my mother's death and had trouble focusing. I decided to go for some coaching for my audition. I was prepared and blissfully calm. I booked the role. I was beyond excited and believed that things were finally turning around. It was now January 2010. The writer's strike was in the past and the economy started to slowly recover.

I was scheduled to be on the set of the show in a week. Unfortunately, the weather did not cooperate. Torrential downpours reigned supreme. Since my scene was outdoors, the producers needed to determine when there would be a break in the weather to be able to shoot outside. My shoot date was pushed up and I had a 5:00 a.m. call time. I was prepared and ready to go. The rehearsal went well. The shoot went well. It felt good to be a working actress. The day before the episode was to air, my manager called to tell me that my scene was cut from the episode.

I could feel my heart sink. I was so disappointed. On the career front, things were looking up. On the spiritual front, I knew I needed help emotionally. I met once a week with a prayer intercessor. She was the opposite of my grandmother. She was elderly with white hair and looked so cuddly. She was gentle and loving, and I just wanted to hug her. There was no judgment, and I felt comfortable speaking openly with her. Her prayers were powerful. They had an impact on my life. I needed to get to the root cause of problems and deal with them. It did not happen overnight, but I started noticing changes in myself. I started coming out of my shell. I started to see the light at the end of the tunnel. I felt loved. I started to believe that God loved me. This was not an overnight revelation. I continued to put one foot in front of the other and believed that I was on the right path, even though many days it felt like I missed the mark.

My spiritual life and my acting life merged. The church implemented a program of connecting people with similar interests into home groups. I started an Arts & Entertainment group. I also volunteered to manage an art exhibit as part of an evening sponsored by Arts & Entertainment Ministries. They felt that my background in management in the beauty industry coupled with my creative acting bent would be a perfect combination to work with the many artists invited to display their work during the evening. I helped the artists set up their displays. It felt good that they trusted my opinion. The evening was such a success, and I loved every minute of it.

Something interesting happened that night into the following week. At the end of the Arts & Entertainment event, I chatted with one of the artists. He looked at me and quoted a line from a popular commercial. He said, "You are like E.F. Hutton. When you talk, people listen." I just looked at him. No one ever said that to me before. I needed to process his comment. The following week, I received a phone call from David Richardson who oversaw the connect groups at church. I trusted him completely, especially when it came to prophetic words. During our conversation, he stopped and said, "You are like E.F. Hutton. When you talk, people listen." That was twice in one week I was told I had something to say, and people listen when I do. I thanked him and said that meant a lot to me.

I sensed I was to attend a conference at church the following weekend. It had to do with SOZO Ministry translated from the Greek word meaning "saved, healed, delivered." I did not want to go. It cost $50 and I was already being ministered to on a weekly basis. In obedience, I went begrudgingly. I went on Friday night grumbling the whole time, "Why am I here?" I went on Saturday morning, again grumbling, "This is a waste of time." I went to the service on Saturday afternoon and sat next to my personal prayer intercessor. She looked at me. I was honest and said, "I don't know why I'm here." At first, she said, "I can tell you don't want to be here." Then she said, "God will show you." I settled in and expected to be frustrated and disappointed.

The speaker for the afternoon was Dawna De Silva, Founder and Co-Leader of SOZO Ministries at Bethel Church in Redding, CA. I never met her and never heard her speak before. She was on the platform. She suddenly stopped and walked down the stairs and up the aisle. As she walked, she pointed her finger at me and said, "Get up." I thought she could not possibly mean me. She stood next to my row and again said, "You, get up." I stood up. She said, "The enemy has been trying to shut you up your whole life. You are like E.F. Hutton. When you speak, people listen. With that, she turned and went back to the platform. The Lord now had my attention.

During this time, I visited a friend of mine once a week at her home. She had a healing ministry and blessed me with her time and her gift of healing. She knew I was strapped for funds, and she refused to let me pay for the sessions. One day, as I laid on her healing table, she had her hands on my stomach. She calmly said, "The enemy has been trying to shut you up your whole life. You're dealing with a spirit of suffocation." She started to rebuke the spirit of suffocation and commanded it to come out of me. There were no histrionics. It was peaceful and calm. That was it. So, I thought.

When I returned home, I started coughing. This was not any ordinary cough. It was from deep within. I continued to cough and cough and cough. I started coughing up bile. This went on for days. Then weeks. Six weeks. I thought I was going to cough up a lung. I was in pain. I thought I broke ribs from all the heavy coughing. I was repulsed by all the bile that was coming up. I called my friend. She explained that the spirit of suffocation was coming out of me. It did not want to leave so a battle was raging. She explained that I had dealt with this my entire life. The Lord was freeing me up. She prayed with me and told me to hang in there. I persevered and made it though. I was exhausted, but I won the battle.

Chapter 12
The Dark Years

On January 30, 2010, that all changed. I was headed to church to lead a prophetic team at the annual Prophetic Conference. I noticed a sea of red lights ahead of me. I realized traffic was stopped so I applied my brake and slowed down. I had plenty of room between my car and the car in front of me. As I came to a stop, I looked in my rearview mirror and saw the car behind me ready to barrel into my car at a high rate of speed. I screamed, "Jesus help me!" In split second timing, I looked in the carpool lane to my left. I did not see any traffic. I turned my car wheel to get into that lane. Everything went into slow motion, as I was rammed from behind. I was propelled into the carpool lane. Everything was a blur. I do not know if I lost consciousness or not. There was such an eerie quiet. I realized I was alive. Somehow, I had the wherewithal to call 911.

I was in a daze. I called Jeanie Richardson since she expected me to arrive for a pre-conference meeting. I needed to let her know what happened. She immediately prayed and told me she was going to gather the intercessors on my behalf. The next thing I remember was a woman stood next to my car. She was on a cellphone. Then the police arrived. I just sat in my car. I was not sure if I could move. One of the policemen approached my car and asked me to open the driver's side window. We chatted for a few moments, and I was able to get out of my car. He asked me if I wanted to go to the hospital. Since I was more lucid and was able to walk, I declined. He asked if I was able to drive the car off the freeway onto the service road. I said, "Yes." The police stopped traffic, and I made my way to the exit. I distinctly remember that the woman who hit my car stood on the side of the service road and continued to talk on her cellphone. I walked over to her and asked if I could pray for her. She said yes. I was not sure what to do next. I had just come from a chiropractic appointment. I thought the accident undid that adjustment, so I called the doctor's office again. He advised me to come back on Monday. It was too soon after the accident to determine what injuries, if any, I sustained. I made an appointment. Thinking back to the events of that day, I should have accepted the officer's suggestion to go to the hospital. I had no idea how injured I was.

I kept my commitment to lead the prophetic team at the conference. I was on automatic pilot When I make a commitment, I keep it. I was greeted by Jeanie and the intercessors. Every part of my body hurt. As the day progressed my body started to feel the effects of the accident. I do not take medication, but I took some Tylenol to ease the pain. I made it home. I did not venture out of the house until my doctor's appointment on Monday.

I only remember one question the doctor asked me during the examination. "How do you feel?" My answer was, "I feel foggy." I did not answer this hurts or that hurts. It was simply, "I feel foggy." I did not know how relevant that statement would prove to be. After a thorough exam, my doctor determined nothing was broken, but I sustained multiple injuries to my neck and back. It took months of treatment. Then, the underlying injuries started to surface. I could not walk. I had so much pain in my right foot that I could not even stand on it. The fogginess continued. I was panicked and hyperventilated. I could not focus. I could not think straight. I did not know what to do. The one thing I knew was that I was injured. I decided it was prudent to retain a personal injury attorney. I was a member of a legal group. I received a call from an attorney a few hours later. I assumed that he was a personal injury attorney. He was not. I learned later that he was a real estate attorney. Apparently, an attorney from any specialty can take on a case. I needed an advocate. Instead, I got an incompetent attorney. I did not know that once I hired an attorney, I could not fire him, even if he is not doing his job. I was required to pay him from any settlement. No other attorney would take the case. I needed my attorney to recommend me to doctors. He did not. I needed my attorney to negotiate paying doctor bills. He did not. I needed my attorney to work with my insurance company to work through my claim. He did not. I was in a situation that spiraled downward and out of control. The medical bills racked up, and I paid them all out of pocket.

I needed to address the pain in my right foot. This reality became more evident when I made my way to an audition on the lot of Fox Studios. I needed to walk the entire length of the studio lot to get to my audition. By the time I arrived, I was in tears. I found the ladies' room and broke down. I managed to pull myself together. I willed myself to audition. I limped back across the studio lot to get to my car. The pain was excruciating. When I reached my car, I broke down.

I called my primary care physician and was told I needed to see a podiatrist. I got the news that I suffered nerve damage in my right foot. The podiatrist said the only option was a localized steroid shot. I freaked out. All I heard was steroid. I am still dealing with the physical and emotional fallout from the steroids I took in Memphis so many years before. I am gripped by fear at the thought of taking medication, especially steroids. My fear is well founded since I have experienced serious side effects from any medication. I refused to take the shot. The doctor assured me that the shot would be local, and the medication would not enter my bloodstream. The need to relieve the pain won out. I took a deep breath and agreed to get the shot.

It was going from bad to worse. I noticed that I could not read. This hit me hard because I was a voracious reader. I was only able to read one line and I did not understand what I read. I, also, noticed that I could not remember anything. My ability to memorize and focus were non-existent. That did not bode well for me as an actress. This became painfully clear when I auditioned for and booked a role for the TV show Greek. I struggled to understand the director's direction. I lost my bearings on set and could not focus. Thankfully, I made it through the shoot.

I noticed that I could not recognize where I was. I got lost in locations I knew well. I went to a mall and parked my car in the garage. When I returned to the parking garage, I was turned around. I did not remember where I parked my car. I did not remember what level I was on. I would always say, "If you do not want me to remember something, don't tell me." This was no longer the case. I stood in the middle of the garage and started to cry. I cried a lot. I knew I was in trouble. This reality was amplified when I went to make myself a cup of tea. Instead of placing the tea kettle on the stove, I placed the plastic water filtration container on the burner. Within minutes, the smoke alarms started ringing and black smoke billowed from the stove as the plastic melted in the fire. It took a while for me to realize what I did. I could have burned the entire apartment down or worse. Lastly, I would look right at something and not see it. I spiraled downward for two and half years. I was in a desperate place. I was ill. I was running out of money. I felt so lost and alone. I needed help. I cried out to God.

My cry for help was answered. An insurance specialist and consultant who worked with attorneys contacted my "attorney" as a networking opportunity. My "attorney" told him about my case, and he referred him to me. We met. He became my advocate. He became the one who dealt with my "attorney." Not me. He also developed a plan for me to receive proper medical attention and diagnosis.

I went to a prayer meeting. There was a woman there that I had met before. She came over to me and asked me, "Have you been in a car accident." I just looked at her. "Why do you ask?" She said, "I see a dark cloud on your brain. This indicates to me that you have had an accident." We started talking and I explained my situation to her. Miraculously, she was a specialist in neurofeedback. I had no idea what neurofeedback was. She explained that neurofeedback retrains the brain to work more efficiently. Since I approach my health holistically, I decided to pursue it. I went for a consultation and initial testing on April 7, 2012. The standard deviation results for my age group revealed that my cognitive skills were severely impacted by the accident. The graph below visually demonstrates that my cognitive skills were well below average.

Response Time Histogram – Totals – April 7, 2012*

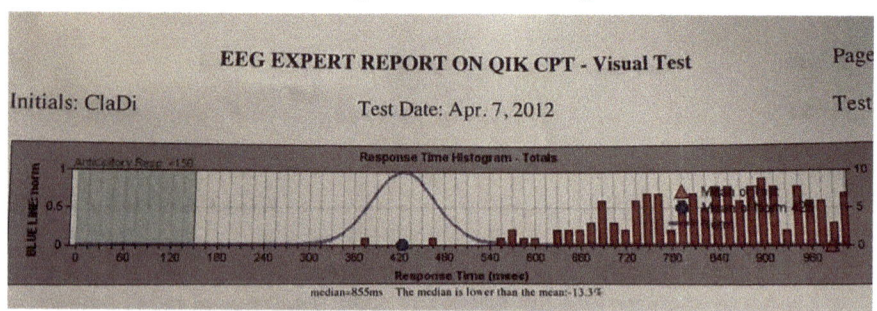

1. **Omission Errors** are significantly greater than average, indicating significant inattention (Low Sustained Attention)

2. **Response Time** is significantly slower than average, indicating significantly low response to targets (low Speed of Response)

3. **Variability of Response Time** is significantly greater than average, indicating significant inconsistency in responding to targets (low Consistency of Response)

*Footnote: Brain Boosters April 8, 2012, Diagnostic Report

A chill ran through me when I realized thatI should not have been driving. Yet, I drove over an hour each way to receive treatments. The Lord truly protected me. While I received treatment; the owner of the company recommended that I see a neurologist. It was then that I discovered that I suffered a concussion from the accident that went undiagnosed and untreated for over two years. I was also diagnosed with PTSD. That explained my emotional outbursts and the panic I felt when a car would get too close to mine. The neurologist suggested that I work with a psychologist to help restore my cognitive abilities. The insurance consultant recommended a psychologist to me. The psychologist administered some preliminary tests to measure my cognitive skill set. Her test results confirmed the results from the neurofeedback EEG testing.

I was a stranger. I did not recognize myself. I was on a mission to be normal. I received neurofeedback treatments on a weekly basis, and I met with the psychologist once per week. I started to show improvement. Then, one day, she told me that I needed to accept that I was permanently disabled. I freaked out. I bolted up out of my seat and said, "I am not disabled. I deal with some disabilities, but do not label me as disabled." I learned to speak words of life over myself. I would not let anyone speak negative words when I could not walk after my leg was healed. I got home and the battle began. I prayed. I worshipped. I spoke the word of God. I returned the following week for my scheduled appointment. My immediate assessment of my therapist was that she did not quite know how to handle me. I started the conversation. I was calm and measured. I explained, "I do not see myself as disabled. I trust that God can heal me. I must do my part, but I believe God's word that by the stripes of Jesus I am healed." Things got quiet for a moment. I could not be swayed. It hit me that I had grown in my faith. I started to look to God and not my circumstances. I spoke up. I used my voice to declare what I believed.

In September, I had a follow up appointment with the neurologist. Even though I was still undergoing neurofeedback treatments, he recommended that I be tested cognitively at a major neuropsychology clinic. This would be relevant in dealing with insurance companies, as neurofeedback was not a traditionally recognized form of medical treatment. I went to the clinic and was tested on three different occasions in September and October. The results showed that I had improved from the testing in April. There were still areas that needed to be treated. The test results did indicate that "I was functioning cognitively, but I was still challenged in performing tasks that required divided attention, as well as processing speed when tasks increased in complexity. I was also dealing with anxiety and moderate depression. I refused to take any antidepressants. It was recommended that I continue with psychotherapy which included education on addressing stressors and coping skills. I also needed to focus on devices that would facilitate memory and recall. I also needed to engage in environments with minimal distractions considering diminishment and processing speed and attention. I needed education and train myself to handle more complex tasks.**

**Footnote: Neuropsychology Outpatient Clinic Neurological Evaluation

Report

I was on the mend, but I had a lot of work ahead of me. In October, I was retested after 60 neurofeedback sessions. The results were remarkable.

I was within normal range on every measure. My neurofeedback therapist told me that such swings were not possible if my cognitive abilities did not exceed the normal range before the accident.

Response Time Histogram Totals – October 13, 2012

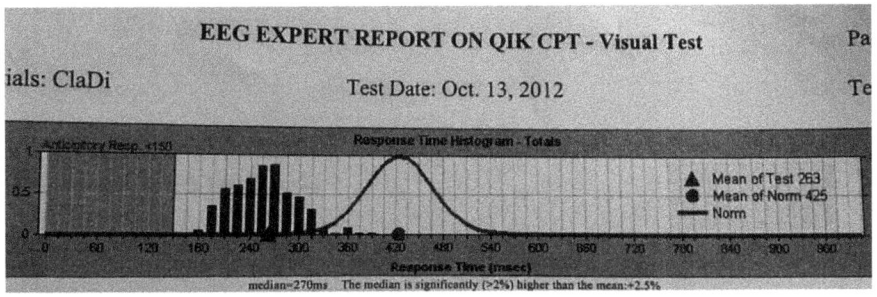

1. **Omission Errors** all scores within the normal range.

2. **Response Time** all scores within the normal range/

3. **Variability of Response Time** all scores within the normal range.

I was on the road to recovery. I still dealt with PTSD and my therapist helped me to work through the trauma. I struggled with the fact that I was emotional. I could swing from joy and laughter to tears and despair within minutes. I also struggled with the fact that I seemed to go on rabbit trails. I used to be focused and could just get to the point. Now I was random, and I seemed to be all over the place. She explained that I had to embrace the new me. She said I received a left frontal lobe brain injury and it triggered other parts of my brain that were not as active as before. She said, "As an actress, you've been given a gift." I looked at her and said, "A gift. What gift?" She explained that the creative side of me has been triggered. She said, "You had great comedic timing before, but now, your comedic timing is flawless. You are like the female Robin Williams.." I did not understand. She said that my rabbit trails were streams of consciousness where I would just flow. She said, "You no longer have a filter. Whatever you are thinking, that is what comes out." That was a scary thought. As time went on, I discovered that people attributed my "tell it like it is" personality to my being from New York. Because I no longer have a filter, I marvel at how I can access my emotions as an actress. I truly live in the moment.

I not only dealt with all this emotional trauma but with the physical fallout from the accident, as well. I was in so much pain in my neck and back. I had come so far and now I had gone backwards. My life revolved around doctors' appointments. I saw the chiropractor three times per week. I was also faced with the reality of the nerve damage in my right foot. My gait was seriously affected, and I did not walk properly. It was now, not just my foot that was painful, but my entire right leg. This upset me terribly. My right leg was healed by God over ten years before. My primary care physician recommended that I see a physical therapist. I went for my consultation, and lo and behold, I needed to strengthen my leg. My physical therapist worked me hard, but he was a Christian, and we talked about the Lord. We encouraged each other.

I screamed in pain. Now my left leg needed physical therapy. The diagnosis was that my left leg overcompensated for my right foot and leg. I moved into a dark place. I felt that God abandoned me. I did everything He asked me to do. I had been through so much already. To make matters worse, my finances dried up. How could God let all of this happen to me? My frustration turned into anger. Yet, He is the center of my world. I could not turn my back and walk away. God where are you?

Chapter 13
Will the Dark Days Ever End

I was on financial fumes. I paid everything out of pocket, and it added to my stress. I needed a job, but I could not read. I could not remember. I could not walk. Who would hire me? I received a call from a friend of mine who joined a financial company. He was my former writing coach and he had shifted gears and became a financial advisor. I met with him about my own finances. Through the company, I learned how to better invest what I had left. I was pleased with the results, and in 2011 I decided to join the company and pursue my license as a life insurance agent with the goal of getting licensed in securities. Did I pray about this? No. I let my panic about money rule my decision. I struggled. My cognitive difficulties were evident. Whenever I attended meetings, I felt as if I was under water. I could not focus. I could not hear anyone. I struggled to study for the licensing exam. I had to repeat and repeat and repeat what I was learned. Thankfully, I passed the test on the first try, but the PTSD was evident. I had a short fuse. This was a major negative in dealing with people. I realized I made a mistake. On the positive side, the people I referred to the company were helped, and I got a better understanding of investing in the market. I learned the mistakes I made in responding to financial loss during the crash of 2008.

My IRA became my financial lifeline. It dwindled. I did not know what to do. My whole life I tried to follow the rules and I am still lost. I was depressed and angry. I was angry at my life. I was angry at my circumstances. I was angry at God. I did my best to live as God wanted me to live. I fell into that place that I was being punished. Only, I did not know what I did wrong. Did I miss God when I moved to Los Angeles to pursue acting? Nothing was going right. I did not know how I was going to make it.

One day, I talked to my medical insurance agent. She listened to my tale of woe. She recommended that I file for disability. That hit me hard. But I was at the point I had to do something. I did my best to fill out the paperwork to apply for disability. I set up an appointment and met with one of the administrators. Within a few weeks, I got the bad news. I was denied disability. I was then informed by my "advocate" that everyone gets denied disability the first time. He recommended an attorney who specialized in disability cases. We met and he took over the case. It was a roller coaster ride.

It was now 2014 and things started to move along with my legal case. I had to attend depositions with the insurance companies. I had never been through a deposition before. The first deposition was with my own insurance company. My attorney was worthless. It was my insurance "advocate" who guided me through the process. I did .my best. What I did not understand was that I had an underinsured rider in my policy for $100,000. The woman who hit my car was underinsured. My own insurance company did not compensate me from my own policy.

My insurance company required me to go for medical evaluations through their recommended doctors. I went through another battery of psychological testing, and I also saw an orthopedist to examine my foot. In their reports, they basically said I was lying. was in pain and had difficulty functioning, I was beside myself. They did not honor my insurance policy. I had to deal with the defendant's insurance company to get compensated, and as I said, she was underinsured.

I attended the deposition for the defendant. Again, my attorney was worthless. She blatantly lied in the deposition. She said she did not have "her" cell phone. I saw her talking on a cellphone when she stood by my car and when we were moved to the service road. She was asked if she was on any medications. She said no. I pressed my attorney to push her. I insisted we step out of the room to talk about her testimony. We wound up in a screaming match. When we went back in the room, he started to question her about medication. She finally admitted that she was bipolar and was on medication. She could not remember if she took her medication that day. Then, she said she had her boyfriend's cellphone. She originally said she did not have "her" cellphone. It was obvious this deposition was going downhill for the defendant. Suddenly, there was a settlement offer. The only problem was her policy maximum did not cover my past, current or future medical expenses.

I felt that everything was against me. I went for my second disability hearing. I was denied. I thought about all the people who cheat the system and get away with it. I had a legitimate claim, and I was denied benefits. I went for a third hearing. Again, I was denied. It was over. I could not apply for another hearing. I did everything I knew to do. That was the problem. I focused on my circumstances. I did pray, but I looked to the world for answers.

I needed God. I needed to humble myself and ask Him to forgive me for being angry with Him. I started to understand having a relationship with the Lord. I was angry with Him, but He was not angry with me. He let me be me. He let me work through it. I needed some sense of stability in my life, yet I sensed the Lord wanted me to leave Harvest Rock Church. That was hard for me. But I left and moved to the church I sensed the Lord wanted me to attend. During my first Sunday visit, the pastor came up to me after the service and said, "There is a prophetic anointing on your life." He then asked me to pray for someone which turned into a prophetic word. The man had to be over 6'5" and I am 5' 2". I started to pray for him, and the Holy Spirit took over. I started to prophesy. Then, the pastor stepped in and said, "I have been telling you this for years, and now God brings in this little woman to tell you the same thing. When will you get it?" I was uncomfortable with the way he talked to the man, but I was grateful that he recognized the gift in me. I thought maybe the Lord moved me to this church because it was smaller. I was catapulted front and center. I was trained. I was ready. I served in what was familiar. I attended intercessory prayer meetings, and I taught Sunday School. I felt accepted and I grew spiritually. I was being trained to hear God's voice in a new way. I no longer had a filter. The channel to God did not have the static it did before. I heard more clearly, but I still wondered if I heard Him or was it me.

I flowed with the Holy Spirit. I was respectful and followed church protocol when I sensed I was to release a prophetic word. I would go to the front of the church and wait to be recognized. This fit right into my early training in Catholic School where I needed to be acknowledged before I could speak or enter a room. One Sunday morning, the Lord used me to release a prophetic word. It was not received well. Individuals approached the pastor after service and complained. The words rang loud as I had heard them before. "Who does she think she is to speak about God wanting to release joy in the church." That statement stung since I had received two prophetic words from people in that very church that the Lord was going to use me to release joy. The pastor did not speak with me. I was punished. I was prohibited from prophesying for two weeks. I cried out to the Lord. I sought Him. From the time I realized I moved in the prophetic gifting, my prayer has been "Lord, fill my mouth and shut it when You are finished." I did not want to speak anything that was not led by the Holy Spirit.

I knew deep down that the Holy Spirit was speaking through me. I needed to understand why I was rebuked when I released a word of joy. I prayed for the Lord to guide me. He did. It was not the prophetic word about joy. It was the way it came through me. The Lord revealed the Greek word "ekstasis". It is a state of ecstasy. It means "amaze, astonish, wonder." This revelation helped me understand why I do not remember the words I release. They are not my words but the Lord's words. As a rule, churches record prophetic words when they are released. I know the word had to do with joy because I was overcome with the joy of the Holy Spirit, and the pastor later referenced the word was about joy. The Holy Spirit put me on a friend's heart, and she called me. This was the friend the Lord used to bind the spirit of suffocation a few years before. She confirmed what I sensed was from the Lord and she encouraged me not to have anyone silence my voice. She said that I heard from God. I did not know what to do next.

I did not run away. I did not withdraw. I waited on the Lord to vindicate me. I was obedient and did not prophesy in the church. The following Sunday the pastor's wife came over and sat down next to me after the service had ended. She told me that the Lord had shown them that they were wrong. She said, "What have we done to you?" She asked me to forgive them. I did so without hesitation, but I was reluctant to step out from that point onward. They were loving people and they treated me like family. They were supportive as I tried to make my way through the drama in my life. I started to have a sense of familiarity.

Then it hit me. They were like my pastors in New York. They had strong personalities, especially the husband. I was being tested.

I passed the test. Once I did, I sensed the Lord was moving me on again. Studying the Word of God has always been a priority in my life. I found it difficult to read the scriptures since the accident. The verse, "Faith cometh by hearing and hearing by the Word of God" (Romans 10:17, KJV) took on new meaning. I felt strongly that I wanted to understand the Hebraic roots of my faith. I attended a bible study with a Messianic Rabbi. I was so blessed by his teachings and how he was used to illuminate the scriptures from a perspective I had never seen before. The Lord wanted me to attend his church. I moved on with a blessing from my pastors.

I attended faithfully, yet I struggled with all the chaos in my life. I needed pastoral guidance. The rabbi agreed to meet with me. After we spoke, he gave me advice I did not expect. He told me to talk to my father about my financial situation. How could I tell my father that the reality of going on welfare loomed large? My family members were products of the Great Depression. They were proud and never took "relief." I felt like a failure on steroids. I was resistant. How could I face my father and ask him to help me? The rabbi assured me that my father loved me, and it would okay. I prayed for the courage to speak to my father.

I sucked it up. I called my father. I broke down. Just as he was there for me when I needed help with my schoolwork, he hit another home run. He offered to give me money each month to help me through. He said that it would come out of my future inheritance, and it would need to be paid back when the time came. He said, "you are my daughter. I love you. I'm here for you." The amount he gave me each month helped tremendously. It did not quite cover my expenses. There was usually more month than money. But somehow, I made it through each month.

I was grateful for the rabbi's advice, and I continued to attend his church which was in Malibu. I discovered Malibu when I first moved to Los Angeles. It is my quiet place with God. I was used to the crowded dirty beaches in Brooklyn and the brown water of the Atlantic. The beauty of Malibu overwhelmed me. The water is blue. The sky is blue. The beaches are not crowded, and the sand is white. I found my spot overlooking Pacific and the coastline. I have traveled to many places around the world, but the beauty of Malibu deeply touches and refreshes me, and I thoroughly enjoyed going there each week. I hoped that I had found a home. I did not like moving from church to church. I wanted stability. My time at the church lasted only ten months. It was then I realized I had been given an assignment. I did not even know it until it was finished. From the first Sunday I attended, I focused on the worship team. The music was good, but, in my spirit, I felt it was more like entertainment than pure worship. I prayed constantly for the true heart of worship. Suddenly, the worship team disbanded. A new group of people joined together without much notice and led worship. It was heavenly. It was then I got the sense I was to leave. I prayed about where I was going next. I received a quick answer. The Lord moved me back to the church I left ten months earlier. This time the assignment was me.

I returned and talked with the pastors to ensure we were on the same page about things. We were, but that did not last long. Once again, I was chastened for a prophetic word I gave in church. I had a long talk with the pastor, and it seemed that we resolved the issue. We did not. I was told I would not be able to prophesy. A teaching rang loudly in my heart that I heard from a pastor at a church I simultaneously attended on Saturdays. I was on a mission to understand how Judaism and Christianity were linked. I attended Breath of the Spirit Ministries with Dr. Michelle Corral as pastor. Her sermons were so powerful and anointed. Each week I felt the Lord spoke directly to me. She was warm and welcoming, and I grew spiritually. I feasted on the meat of the Word and not milk. In one of the sermons, Dr. Corral explained how she had to respect the anointing in her life. She was a guest speaker at a church and was asked to change her sermon. It did not quite fit the tenets of the church. She did not bow to man. She decided to honor God and the anointing in her life. She never spoke at that church again.

That sermon resonated deep within me. The Lord moved me back to that church to learn a valuable lesson. I decided I could not let anyone quench the anointing on my life. I left the church and attended Breath of the Spirit Ministries under Dr. Michelle Corral for seven years. The teaching and preaching were powerful. I learned so much. Although it felt like my life was in shambles, my spiritual life prospered, and I was filled to overflowing. I started to see that I needed to do more than just read the bible. I needed to study it. I needed to unearth the deep revelations that knitted the scriptures together. I started to see that there are no coincidences. I was on a journey to understand my faith and how the Lord is personal and speaks through His Word. This truly helped me cope with everything going on in my life. Dr. Corral then started The Institute of Hebraic Studies through Melodyland School of Theology. Bells rang. I knew I was to study the Torah. I was concerned about my challenge with reading and comprehension.

Miraculously, I was able to study the depth of the scriptures and understand what I read. My eyes were opened to see Jesus from Genesis through Revelation and understanding the importance of the Jewish feasts and God's appointed times and seasons. I studied for four years. The bible is no longer a book. It is the living Word. Looking back, I believe the Lord planted a seed in me to hunger for His Word when He met me in Israel almost thirty years before.

The more I studied, the more the Lord refined my character. My legal battle was over, but I continued to harbor a deep anger toward my attorney. I prayed about bringing him before the California Bar Association. It would take resolve and energy to move in that direction. The more I thought about it the angrier I got. Then, the Lord used Dr. Corral to answer my prayer. Dr. Corral preached on Abraham and Lot and Isaac and the Philistines. To avoid strife, Abraham allowed Lot to choose the land he wanted. Lot chose the best land. They went their separate ways. The Lord prospered Abraham (Genesis Chapter 13). Isaac kept building wells, and the Philistines would lay claim to each well when it was finished. Instead of going to battle with the Philistines, Isaac allowed them to take the wells. The Philistines recognized that the Lord was with Isaac, and they made a covenant with Isaac that there would be no hurt between them. Isaac prepared a feast for them. (Genesis Chapter 26). I sobbed through the sermon. I got the message loud and clear, but I had to work through my emotions. I was obedient. I did not bring my attorney before the Bar Association. I could not allow strife to rule my life. I needed to move forward. I needed to let go of anger. I needed to have peace. I needed to forgive. It was not easy. I battled to let go of anger and move on. I battled to find my peace. I battled to forgive. My emotions raged inside of me. I needed to let them out. I needed to heal.

The creative side of my brain had been activated. I started to heal through poetry. I never wrote poetry. I never liked poetry. I was on a roller coaster ride of emotion. I poured out my soul. I allowed myself to feel what I was feeling.

There Are Days

There are days I look up and say thank you.

There are days I look up and ask why.

There are days I lift my hands and worship With abandon and tears streaming down from my eyes. There are days I croak out scripture knowing that I need to battle to change my place.

My place of confusion.

My place of pain.

My place of wondering where You are.

There are days my circumstances overwhelm me.

There are days I know when I am weak You are made strong.

I've come to a place of being totally dependent.

Knowing of myself I can do nothing.

I need only believe that I can do all things through You.

I need only trust that You will guide me and teach me.

I need only die to myself and my struggle to surrender.

I am called a woman of God.

Yet, there are days I feel like a fraud.

There are days I am a warrior.

Today, I come before you and cry out for help.

Help to stand strong.

Help to stir myself up.

Help to know that You are in control.

Help to know that You have a plan.

Let my tears water the seeds of my destiny.

Help me be the overcomer I know that I am.

Help me rest in You, the Great I AM.

Claudia DiMartino - 3/16/13

Chapter 14

Trust Is a Choice

I was no longer the person I knew so well. I was changed physically, emotionally, and spiritually in one driver's reckless moment behind the wheel. I struggled to embrace the changes in me. Writing a poem was not the same thing as pounding the pavement. It seemed frivolous. I needed to be responsible. I no longer knew how. I was no longer the "ruffiana," the free spirit. I was lost and struggled to find my way back. I battled to come out from under the weight of life. I lived day to day. My only plan was to get healthy and seek the Lord. The most crushing blow was that I could not provide for myself financially. So much of my identity was caught up in being financially independent. It was as if a sledgehammer was taken to my financial wall. It crashed down around me. I struggled to ask for help from the one person I could trust, my father. Without hesitation, he did what a father does. He loved me. He provided for me. He was the living embodiment of the Father heart of God. I could trust my father. Why could I not trust God? I was at a crossroads. I knew I had faith. But I realized that faith is a gift, and trust is a choice. I chose to jump off a cliff and into the arms of my heavenly Father.

The Lord gave me a vision of my destiny. I had to trust that He would get me there. To move forward, I needed to let go of the past. I was in the process of healing, but physical and emotional wounds went deep. The last few years stripped me of myself. I felt crushed. Then I remembered a study I did about olives. To release the oil from an olive, the olive must be crushed twice. The first crushing is to break the skin. The second crushing is to release the oil. I needed the oil of the Holy Spirit to flow. I remembered a sermon I once heard about eagles. When eagles are wounded, they go into the cleft of the rock to heal. Other eagles, who have gone through the healing process, protect them. Inside the cleft of the rock, they break their beaks and pull out their feathers. Oil is emitted. When the eagle is healed, it emerges from the cleft of the rock and can fly higher and see further than it did before. I saw myself as an eagle and my rock is Jesus. I needed time to let the Lord heal me and rely on the oil of the Holy Spirit to comfort me and bring me through. As I sheltered in the cleft of the rock, I searched my soul. Looking deep, I realized, to let go of the past, I needed to forgive. I said I forgive so many times. This time was different. Forgiveness had to come from the depths of me. It was a painful ordeal. Poetry became my outlet to release the pain. It was no longer trivial. Poetry became a gift from God that enabled me to truly let go.

I Forgive

I feel a war raging inside of me Where is this coming from?

Open my heart so I can see

See into the depths of my soul

There is such an intensity within me

I yearn to be free

Free from those things that would bind me

Free from wounds created long ago

People have come in and out of my life

There are those who have caused so much strife

I thought I let go

Yet faces of the past flash before my eyes

Tears start streaming down my face

I've been here before

I know the pain of betrayal

Like a dagger, lies from those I trusted cut deep

I toss and turn in my sleep

As I look for answers

But I know the truth

I look at myself and I cannot escape

My eyes are the window of my soul

So many times, I have rerun the tape

And said the words and felt sorrow lift

But, once again, I am humbled to the core

I need to forgive

The time is now to truly let go

So, through tears and a contrite heart

I forgive those I love

I forgive those I respected

I forgive those who turned away

But mostly, I forgive myself

For condemning myself and believing lies that have held me back
from all I can be I choose to be free. I choose my destiny.

And yes, once and for all, I choose to lay down all that is death. I
choose to live.

I choose to forgive.

Claudia DiMartino – August 22, 2013

Forgiveness is not an overnight event. It is a process. At least, I
took the first step and allowed myself the grace to move through it. My
onion had a lot of layers that needed to be peeled back. The deeper I
went, the stinkier it got. I had to face the reasons why I resisted trusting
God so much, especially in my finances. As I mentioned, my family
was a product of the depression. Without question, things were tight.
During those years, my grandmother would call out to my mother to
see how much money her husband left for the day. Sometimes it was

a penny, sometimes two cents, sometimes nothing. Even though my grandmother worked as a seamstress in the garment center in New York City, there was never enough. My mother grew up with that depression mentality. Of all the children in the house, I think it had the most impact on me. I grew up feeling like there was never enough. There was always food on the table, and we did get to go out and enjoy family entertainment and simple vacations. But I remember my mother pinching pennies and budgeting to the exact cent each week. My dad was a good provider, but still waters run deep. When I grew up, I was always concerned about not having enough. I had good jobs that paid well. I was a saver. My splurge was traveling, but I made sure I saved up to pay for each vacation. I did not believe in carrying debt.

As life happened and I faced financial crisis after financial crisis, I needed to understand why I struggled. I got spiritual guidance, I got prayer to break strongholds and generational curses. I tried to get to the cause of my struggles. To me, it seemed like I was the only one out of my sister and cousins who had this problem. I did all I knew to do, yet I still struggled. As an actress, I was not exactly pulling in enough income to sustain me. I had auditions and I booked some roles, but they were few and far between. I had a fear of being destitute even though I seemed to make it through each month. I had a fear of being punished. My mindset was performance based. If I did something wrong, I would be punished. I had to learn that "There is no fear in love. But perfect love drives out fear because fear has to do with punishment. The one who fears is not made perfect in love." (1 John 4:18). I needed to comprehend that God loved me, and I was not going to be struck down by a bolt of lightning from heaven if I made a mistake. I needed to believe that "…my God shall supply all your need according to His riches in glory by Christ Jesus." (Philippians 4:19, NKJV).

It is such a contradiction that I believed that my Father in heaven would punish me and not provide for me. My Dad had a saying, "If people did not make mistakes, there would be no erasers on pencils." He understood that we all make mistakes. The important thing was to learn from them and move on. My Dad was generous. He took his role as father seriously and took care of his children. The strange thing is he had another saying that belied the way he was. He would say, "I will never deny you the right to be poor." As my depth of understanding grew, I recognized that this saying was a curse. With pastoral help, we broke that curse. After that, I asked my dad never to say that to me again. I knew he would not understand that those words were a curse instead of a blessing. I lovingly explained that it was the total opposite of his actions. He simply said, "Okay."

I needed to trust that God's word is true. I needed to understand that I was being molded into the character of God. "But now, O Lord, You are our Father, we are the clay, and You our potter; and all we are the work of Your hand." (Isaiah 64:8, NKJV). As I was being molded, I slowly embraced the new me. I was no longer the no nonsense businesswoman who worked around the clock and lived a life of trying to get ahead. My creative side was blossoming, and I tend to go more with the flow. I am still mindful of time, and I keep my commitments. But I seem to have slowed down. I stop now and smell the roses. Does that come from being changed by the accident or living in California? It does not matter. I now allow myself to experience what is around me. I started to emerge from the cleft of the rock. I had come through. I was stronger. I had a new vision of myself and my relationship with God. I was still a bit shaky, though, about trusting God to provide for me. But one thing was clear. My life had shifted. I felt a convergence happening. I am now not only an actress, but a writer. I needed to express myself.

One day I chatted with a friend. She mentioned that she was taking a free workshop each week where she was learning to develop her own one-woman show. The word "free" rang loud. I asked her for more details, and she invited me to join her at the next class. I thought, "Why not!" I was nervous. I was in uncharted waters. I dabbled in a writing class before and started to write my one-woman show; but this was on a larger scale. The class was held in a theater and class members performed their work on stage. What if I could not write? What if I was fooling myself? What if? What if? What if? How many times have I used those two little words to talk myself out of doing something? Even though I have had to battle fear, I have always said, "I don't want to go to my grave saying I should have." I put things into perspective. I already took the huge step to move to Los Angeles. I battled through a brain injury and cognitive decline. I am reading again. Now I can write. Yes, it is time to step out into the new.

I took my first class in October 2015. I was introduced to Jessica Lynn Johnson, an award-winning writer, performer, director, and teacher who founded Soaring Solo. She generously shared her years of experience developing and producing one person shows. Jessica encouraged us in a loving and encouraging way. Her class was a safe space. It was the environment I needed. Jessica started each class with a writing exercise. She explained the exercise would jumpstart everyone into a creative writing flow. I surprised myself how I was able to write using the exercise as my guide. Students were invited to come up on stage to share their work. I was amazed how willing students were to get up and perform. At first, I observed. I quickly realized that each student had a unique writing style and a way of expressing themselves. This was not cookie cutter. Expressing one's individuality was supported and encouraged. After a few students performed their class writing exercise, the class moved into prepared work. Many students, including my friend, were in the process of developing their shows to perform in SoloFest 2016. SoloFest is the largest festival on the West Coast dedicated to giving a platform to solo show artists. This was an annual event that featured over fifty one-person shows. Students performed scenes or narration from their shows. Jessica gave her critique and then invited those in the class to give their input.

I was blown away. The stories were so personal and expressed with such rawness and truth. As I watched, I felt a flutter of excitement. I thought, "I can do that." I knew this is what I was looking for. I took another step of faith. I made a coaching appointment with Jessica to go through the show I had written a few years before. With script in hand, I did a cold run through of my show. She said it was a great start, but there was opportunity to develop the script and the characters. I agreed to work with Jessica. With her help, I jumped into the deep end of the pool and started to develop my show. The classes were free, but coaching had a price tag attached. I took a hard look at my finances. I scrimped in ways I did not even know I could scrimp. It was worth it.

I got a taste of bits and pieces of solo shows in class. I needed to experience what a full show looked like under Jessica's direction. I had seen one-person shows before, and I walked away asking "why?" I attended my friend's show. That night I was introduced to what a solo performer show should be. I was mesmerized by the professionalism and the high caliber of the writing, the performance, the staging, and the direction. When the show finished, I jumped to my feet gave her a standing ovation. My step of faith took me into a whole new world. I knew I was in the right hands and was now excited about bringing my own show to life. My goal was to premiere my show in SoloFest 2017.

I was invited by Jessica to perform in a showcase in June 2016. The evening would feature fifteen-minute segments from several shows. A full show usually runs around 60-70 minutes. I was now a playwright, producer, and a performer. It was exhilarating. It was also on the job training. I was able to draw on my business skills to coordinate the production side of things. I felt it was miraculous that I could get past my cognitive issues. I was able to write my segment, memorize it and perform it in my show. I learned that repetition was key for me to memorize my lines. I repeated my lines over and over again until they were a part of me.

The day of the showcase arrived. I was overjoyed that many friends came out to support me. I was not nervous. I was in the zone. I knew I wanted to act and booking work for TV and film was thrilling. Being on stage was a new experience. It energized me. When I stepped on stage, I was in my own little world. When I was young, I performed for myself. I was now on stage and was fueled by the live audience and their reactions throughout my performance. I did not know acting could be so much fun. The showcase performance sealed the deal that I would perform in SoloFest. Flying high from my fifteen minutes of fame blinded me to the amount of work and stress involved in putting on a full solo show. It is one thing to be part of a showcase with other performers. I was now on my own and had to dive into the deep end of the pool. The stress level was high. I had to finish writing the show. I needed to take on full producer and administrative responsibilities. I needed to be coached as a performer to ensure that the show would be of the highest caliber. I needed to market and promote my show. Even though I had twenty years of marketing experience behind me, I stressed out because I had to ensure that the theater was sold out. If I did not have enough ticket sales to at least cover the cost of the theater, I had the weight of personally paying for the theater space myself. It was nerve wracking.

As I delved into writing my show, something strange started to happen. I found myself getting very emotional. I had trouble writing. It became clear that I needed to heal from the wounds of the past. I spent many hours broken before the Lord asking Him to go deep and heal me. I moved from pouring myself into poems to heal to now pouring myself into my show. I remember doing one scene in class. It was when my boss told me I laughed too much. I broke down on stage. I could not seem to pull myself together.

The pain of not being able to be myself still lived inside me. Jessica, in her wisdom, suggested I sit down and take some deep breaths. Another student went in my place. After they finished, I was able to get back up on the stage and do the scene. I needed to let it out.

I kept moving forward and prepared for my show which was scheduled to premiere on February 10, 2017. I was focused, then, it felt like the bottom fell out. On November 17, 2016, I called my dad. He did not answer. I called and called and there was no answer. I called my sister. She was also trying to reach him. My brother-in-law decided to go to his apartment to see if he was okay. He was not. My brother-in-law found my father dead on the kitchen floor. He had congestive heart failure. My brotherin-law picked up the phone as I tried to call for the umpteenth time. I recognized his voice and said, "Peter, is everything okay?" I think he was in shock. He abruptly said, "He's gone" and hung up. I just stared at the phone as the news hit me. I broke down. My father, my friend, my confidant, my advisor, my help in time of trouble was gone. I did not even get to say goodbye. It was later that I realized that the loss of my earthly father was the beginning of my journey to allow myself to trust my Father in heaven. Even though I jumped off the cliff with the Lord, my dad was still my safety net. I had no choice now but to look up.

I pulled it together and flew to Connecticut to be with my family. Like my mother, my dad died near Thanksgiving. My sister and Peter made all the arrangements for the funeral. It was small, since most of the family were scattered and unable to come. It was decided to have a memorial service just before the funeral. My sister asked each of us to say something heartfelt. For me, she asked me to do something unusual. I had explained key scenes in my upcoming show to her. She asked me to do the scene where my father raised my allowance after discovering I stole money out of my mother's purse to buy stamps for the missions. I think people were taken by surprise, but it was a microcosm of sharing who my father was. I also shared a poem I had written to him. My sister and I held it together pretty well, until the service moved into a military salute. My father was in the Navy during WWII. In military tradition, a soldier played taps on the trumpet. When they folded the American flag that draped my father's coffin and handed it to my sister, I thought I would lose it. That would come later.

After the service, we went out for lunch and some friends joined us. When my dad retired, he took up cooking and baking, much to the chagrin of my mother. He loved tiramisu. Instead of toasting him with wine, my sister ordered tiramisu for dessert. We all took a forkful and clinked our forks together. I looked over at my sister and just smiled. This day was all too familiar. I flew in on Wednesday, we had a small Thanksgiving dinner on Thursday and the wake and funeral on Friday. Something else was familiar. I never got the chance to mourn the loss of my mother. One month after she died, I was in the car accident. Now, I wanted to mourn the loss of my father. I could not.

I stayed at my father's apartment. I sorted through my father's belongings and tried to organize everything. Suddenly, I heard a key in the lock on the door. I went to see who it was. Management of the complex was informed that my father had passed away, and the maintenance man tried to enter the apartment. He was surprised to see me there. I explained who I was, and I was there to clean things out. He left. The next thing I knew the manager and the maintenance man were at the door. They were there to evict me from the premises. My name was not on the lease and, therefore, I could not stay in the apartment. I tried to explain the circumstances, but the manager did not have any of it. I tried to keep my wits about me. I quickly threw things in my suitcase. I had the wherewithal to retrieve my father's suitcase and grab his files and personal papers. I would not leave his private papers in the apartment unsupervised.

I left with suitcases in tow and drove off in my father's car. I tried to drive in a torrential downpour. I pulled into the parking lot of a supermarket and tried to call my sister. She said she could not talk and to call back later. LATER! I was hysterical. I think my tears matched the heavy rain falling outside. I was cold. I was wet. I was upset. At that moment, I felt so alone. I did not know where to go. I sat in the car for what seemed an eternity. I called my sister back. She explained that Peter was on the phone with the manager and tried to work things out. He could not. My sister told me to come to the house. I made my way through the dark, winding roads in the pouring rain. I took a wrong turn and was lost. I still dealt with spatial recognition issues. I needed to figure out where I was. I was in a remote area, and I could not get reception on my cellphone. I cried out to God to help me. I finally made it to the main road and was able to find my way to my sister's home.

When I entered the house, my sister explained that Peter made some headway with the manager. They agreed to let me back into the apartment for the rest of my stay. I was grateful for Peter's diplomacy, but I was so traumatized that I was hesitant to go back. I did. My stay was emotional. Going through old photographs and memories hit me hard. I tried to get past the trauma and focus on the love my father always showed me. It was so evident even after he died.

During my time in Connecticut, my sister, Peter, and I needed to discuss my father's estate. Things were a bit complicated. He was scheduled to sign his updated will on Monday. He died the Thursday before. Things were not quite as settled as he thought they were. As we sat at the kitchen table, I looked at my sister and Peter. I said, "I know dad withdrew part of my inheritance to help me through these past few years. When the settlement is finalized, I will pay back what I was given." My sister looked at Peter and then at me. She said, "Didn't dad tell you?" Tell me what?" Her next words stunned me. She said, "The loan is forgiven. You do not owe us anything." I could have been knocked over with a feather. I think I was in shock. Then, I broke down at the thought that, even to end, my dad was so generous and took care of me. My gratitude was even greater with the fact that my sister and Peter had no problem with it at all. There were no arguments. There was no contesting it. Without hesitation, they honored my father and his wishes. It really hit home that we are there for each other. It hit home that my father provided for me, and I would be okay.

As I packed my bags and headed back to Los Angeles, I had a great deal to think about. I needed to bounce back from the trauma of the trip. I needed to focus on the wonderful memories with my father and how blessed I was that my dad, as a father, was an example of my Father in heaven. I rejoiced that he was with Jesus in heaven. He asked Jesus into his heart a few years after my mother passed away. I knew I would see him again in heaven. It was time to focus on returning to life. I had to think about my show and finalize all the details. Things were going according to plan. I had found my voice, and I looked forward to doing my show and telling my story. Then, two weeks before my show, the bottom fell out again. CANCER!

Chapter 15
Down but Not Out

With everything I had been through physically, I listen to my body. In 2016, I noticed I was bleeding. I was past that time in my life, and this got my attention. At first, I just monitored the problem. Then I realized this was not going away. I went to the doctor, and she told me I needed to go through a battery of tests to determine the problem. I got a twinge in the pit of my stomach. I had been through so much. The last thing I needed was another medical problem. I submitted to the tests, and they were inconclusive. It was determined that I needed to have a biopsy done. The word biopsy sent shivers throughout my body.

I was grateful I did not have to focus solely on having the biopsy. I agreed to portray Maria Woodworth Etter as part of a series of productions through Breath of the Spirit Ministries featuring the generals in the faith. As I studied Maria's life, I found it fitting that I was chosen to portray her. She was a healing evangelist during the 19th and early 20th centuries. She had been through much hardship. She divorced her first husband for infidelity and lost five of her children to death. She had to depend on the Lord for her strength, and the Holy Spirit always showed up when she ministered to others. She did not give up. I dug deep, and I was consumed with her as I performed two days before the biopsy was scheduled. I was able to draw on my own physical, emotional, and spiritual challenges to bring her to life. As the Holy Spirit was there for her, He was there for me. He filled me up to do what I was called to do. In return, her life encouraged me as I faced another challenge.

I now had to face the biopsy. I was not alone. I asked for prayer from friends and family. I had peace as I headed to the hospital for the 15-minute procedure. I prayed quietly in the spirit and trusted that the Lord was with me. When I woke up, the doctor told me the procedure went well, and I just needed to wait for the results. I went home to recuperate. Even though I believed the results would be negative, it was hard to just wait. The following day I noticed I had difficulty walking. My legs started to swell. They felt funny during the night as I tried to sleep. By the next day, my legs and feet were so swollen I could not put on a pair of shoes. Panic started to set in. I called a friend who lived near me. She and her fiancé rushed me to the emergency room. They stayed with me and prayed over me. As they prayed, they declared that I was healed. Having them there, kept me calm. The swelling started to dissipate. After a few hours it was determined that I had a severe reaction to the anesthesia. I was not surprised. I take a holistic approach to my health. I try and avoid any medication, since I have battled for years to reverse the effects of the steroids that wreaked havoc with my body.

On January 23rd, I received a call from my gynecologist's office. They asked me to come in that day. I thought, "This cannot be good. I arrived and was ushered into an examining room. The doctor finally came into the room. She sat down and in no uncertain terms said, "The biopsy came back positive. You have cancer in the endometrial lining of your uterus." It was like I was gut punched. That word cancer will do that. In my shock I said, "Doctor, that can't be." She then said, "The good news is it's stage one." Still not grasping the news, "What does that mean?" "It means you caught it early." Again, "What does that mean?" "If you are going to get cancer, this is the one to get." "Huh?" She said, "Surgery will take care of everything. The cancer will be completely removed. Most likely, you will not need to go through chemo or radiation." Things started to penetrate my brain. "You're talking about a full hysterectomy?" "Yes." Then I asked a question, "Can I keep my ovaries? I thought what the doctor said next was strange. Now I think it is funny. She said, "Have you used them in a while?" Embarrassed, I said, "No." She said, "They must come out too."

My head was spinning. I held back tears as I tried to process the diagnosis. I should have asked a friend to go with me to the appointment. But it happened so quickly, there was not enough time. I got back to my car. I just sat there. I took a deep breath and asked the Lord to help me drive home safely. When I arrived home, a flood of emotion hit me. In my humanness, I broke down and sobbed. I could not think. I could not speak. All I could focus on was I had cancer. It was not until a few hours later that I remembered the doctor's words, "if you are going to get cancer, this is the one to get. You caught it early. It's stage one." Through my tears, I cried out, "Why God, why? I do not understand why. I have been through so much already." I finally pulled myself together and did what I knew to do. I was not ready to call my sister, who has been with me through thick and through thin. Instead, I called Jeanie Richardson, my prophetic mentor, for prayer. She is one of the few people in my life that I trust completely. She listened. She prayed. She spoke words of life. As she spoke, I felt a peace come over me. I was now ready to deal with what I was facing.

After a few days, it was time to call those closest to me and let them know what was going on. It was amazing. My voice was so calm. I was so calm. I reached the place of trusting God and knowing He did not bring me this far to say, "Oh, just kidding." I know there is a plan for my life. I know my destiny. I knew that I would get through this and be able to get on with my life. When I called my niece who is a nurse, I remember her saying, "Aunt Claudia, you are so calm." I assured her that I was, and I needed to keep things in perspective.

I was ready to focus on my show which was scheduled to open in one week. In the fog of my doctor telling me I had cancer, I asked her, "Can I do my show." She asked me when it was. I told her it was February 10th. Since it was only one night, she said I could do the show. It would take a few weeks to get insurance approvals and meet with the oncologist. I took a deep breath and plowed forward. Except for my director Jessica, I did not tell anyone I was dealing with cancer. I wanted to keep private. I still had to wrap my head around cancer and what I was facing. I had a full schedule. It was a good thing because it kept my mind busy. I went for coaching sessions. I attended classes and worked through scenes from my show. I was diligent in marketing and promoting my show. I planned every detail. As show day approached, I started to get a little nervous. As I prayed, I sensed the Lord say, "Relax, you are dealing with cancer. This show is nothing compared to that. Have a blast."

The day of the show was abuzz with activity. It started with a pleasant surprise. As I was about to leave for the theater, my doorbell rang. My sister and Peter surprised me and sent a beautiful bouquet of my favorite flower, tulips. It was so special. I felt so special. I immediately called to thank them. As I left for the theater, the adrenaline was pumping. Jessica, myself, and my technical director arrived early to go through the technical details of the show such as lighting, sound, and projection. I needed to walk through the show scene by scene to ensure that it all worked well together. This process took about four hours. Then, I did a run through of the entire show. I wanted to feel comfortable that everything flowed. That Type A personality thing does not go away. With all of this going on, I could not oversee the post-show reception. Thankfully, a friend of mine offered to help me with any last minute details. She was, also, the caterer extraordinaire and helped me by setting up all the food, dessert, and beverages I provided.

As the rehearsal ended, I did my final pre-show prep. Jessica and I prayed together on the stage. We invited the Holy Spirit into the theater. I then quietly anointed each seat and doorway with oil. I asked the Lord to bless each person attending the show and to bless the show itself. The only thing left was to wait for showtime. I discovered something about myself as I waited backstage. I was very chatty with my technical director. The tech booth was backstage, and we were both in the waiting mode. I thought I would want to be quiet. I tried putting headphones on to listen to music. That made me nervous. I needed to chat. We got to know each other better, and I felt energized. It was almost showtime, and, on the monitor, I noticed people coming into the theater, but I could not hear them. I asked him to put on the sound. I was exhilarated listening to all the chatter and laughter as people filled the theater. The show was sold out. I eagerly wanted to experience every moment.

I heard the pre-show music begin. I suddenly stopped chatting and went into my zone. I did not realize that would happen. I now needed to get centered. I stretched. I paced. I did my breathing exercises again. It all became real. Jessica and the theater director came on stage to welcome the audience and introduce them to the evening's program. I moved into position behind the curtain. The lights went out. The stage was dark. I took my position on the stage. The moment I stepped foot on the stage the Holy Spirit met me there and took over. It was real and surreal at the same time. The lighting came up and I started to speak. Everything faded away except performing my show. I was transported into pure joy. I found my voice. I told my story and expressed myself my way.

It is as if I danced through my show. I took what the Lord said to heart. I had a blast! The showcase I did the year before was dwarfed in comparison to doing an entire show. I portrayed forty characters from family members to teachers, to employers. I created voices and mannerisms for each one. I did not know I had it in me until I pulled the show together. The show was timed to run about 70 minutes. With audience reactions throughout, the show ran for 90 minutes. I fed off the energy in the audience. I reacted to their reactions. It is an experience I will always remember. I was living my dream on my terms. When the show finished and the lights came up, I came back on stage to take a bow. The moment I came out the audience got to their feet and gave me a standing ovation. I was overwhelmed and overjoyed at the same time. People lined up and waited to offer me their hearty congratulations. They stayed through the Q&A. They stayed for the reception. This show validated that I was doing what I was meant to do. I was not trying to satisfy the little actress in me. I was satisfying me, the woman.

I got home around midnight and could not sleep. I was still on an adrenaline rush. The next day I was physically and emotionally exhausted. But it was the good kind. I gave myself a break. My big event for the day was to call my sister and tell her all about it. She has supported me since the day I told her I started pursuing acting. She has always there for me. As we talked,

I could just feel her heart swell with pride and joy for me. She knew what I was facing and was elated that I was able to do my show without focusing on my diagnosis.

I allowed myself to bask in aftermath of my show for about two days. I gleefully read glowing emails and reviews on social media. Then, it was back to the reality of life. My emotions were tangible. As I focused on my circumstances, the peace I had was gone. My relationship with the Lord had deepened, so much so, I moved from calling Him Father, to Abba, which means Daddy. I allowed myself to be real with Him. I entered my feelings in my journal. I was raw. "Abba, I am glad faith and feelings have nothing to do with each other. I have been in a very difficult place emotionally concerning the stage 1 cancer diagnosis. Now that my show premier is done, my focus has shifted to the surgery and what I am dealing with now. I have been very emotional and crying. I do not understand what you are trying to teach me now. Is it to trust you more? Is it just to stand and believe? I feel I am at the place where I cannot bear anymore. And I am asking you to provide a way of escape. It has been very hard to pray and close in with you. I feel so alone. But I know the truth of Your Word that You will never leave me or forsake me. I declare Your Word. Greater is He that is in me than he that is in the world. Daughter, thy faith has made thee whole. Go in peace and be whole of thy plague. Blessed am I who believe for there will be a performance of those things told to me of the Lord. By the stripes of Jesus, I am healed. I know you love me Lord. I need a hug. I really need to be held." Since the accident, my faith was strengthened by hearing the word of God. Now, as I poured out my emotions by writing the scriptures down, I was uplifted past my pain. In my weakest moments, I come around when I use the power of God's Word to bring me through. I did receive a hug. The Lord gave me the strength to do what I needed to do.

I prepared for the surgery. I dealt with the insurance. I saw the oncologist who confirmed the need for surgery. I also did something that was not in the normal course of events. The bad reaction I had to anesthesia after a 15-minute procedure was fresh on my mind. I did not want to go through that again. I was facing a two-hour surgery and would be knocked out for a much longer length of time. I called the acupuncturist who helped me deal with allergies in the past. Through her holistic approach to health, she said she could treat me for allergies to both anesthesia and antibiotics. Antibiotics are given to patients who have surgery as a precaution against infection. I needed to protect myself from the onslaught of medication that would be pumped into my body. It was wise for me to see her. I tested weak for both anesthesia and antibiotics. After I was treated, she tested me again. I no longer showed weakness. She said that I would be able to handle the surgery well. I breathed a sigh of relief.

I was now subjected to the pre-op examination. Things were going well until an intern had difficulty administering the EKG. The little suction cups kept falling off. I am sure it affected the outcome of the test. I was told the results indicated that I needed to see a cardiologist. That did not sit well with me. I said, "Why? I had an EKG six weeks ago and everything was fine." Things were down to the wire. The surgery was scheduled for March 8th. I was supposed to see the cardiologist the week before, but there was a big mix up with the referral. My primary care doctor had to get involved and called the cardiologist directly. I was given an appointment on March 6th. After being examined by the cardiologist, he said that I needed to go for a stress test. I told him that I was scheduled for surgery on Wednesday. He said I should postpone it. I glazed over as I tried to process what he told me. I held it together until I got to my car. I broke down. I called a friend for prayer. She suggested I call my oncologist to explain what was happening. I did. I spoke to his assistant and did my best to explain the situation. She said she would alert him to the problem. I heard back from the doctor's office. He was surprised that I would be given another EKG, since I had one six weeks before which was fine. He felt there would not be a problem. I was in a quandary. Should I postpone the surgery and get the stress test, or should I rely on the EKG results from six weeks earlier and keep the surgery scheduled?

My being human answered the question. The stress started to get to me. On Tuesday, I started to hyperventilate and bleed more heavily. I thought my heart was going to come out of my chest. I called the oncologist's office. It was suggested I get myself to the emergency room. My friends picked me up and drove me to the hospital. I did not know what would happen, and in the throes of all of it, I packed a bag. When I got to the emergency room, they took my vitals. My blood pressure was through the roof. It did not come down. They called my doctor. The decision was made to check me into the hospital that night instead of the next day. My oncologist said he would call the Head of Cardiology at the hospital to discuss my situation.

I was admitted and brought to my room which was in the oncology ward. I could feel a heaviness in the air. I was the only patient in the ward that was ambulatory. I did not have a peaceful night's sleep. My roommate had many visitors who came in shifts and were very loud. I was also diagnosed with a bladder infection, so I needed to go to the bathroom every half hour. I was on a drip and was instructed by the nurse to take the pole and the drip with me whenever I needed to use the bathroom. At about two in the morning, I made my way to the bathroom with pole and drip in hand. The nurse came in and asked me what I was doing. I told her I was going to the bathroom. She said, "Why are you bringing your pole and drip?" I said, "I was instructed to do so." She just looked at me and said, "We unhooked you about an hour ago." I felt the donkey ears sprout. I must have drifted off to sleep at some point and did not realize I could move around feely. There is nothing like real life to give fodder for comedic relief. It did not stop with the pole. Every time I got up to use the bathroom, I would trigger the automatic hand towel dispenser. My head was directly in line with the activation signal. By the time the morning came, the dispenser had jammed. Maintenance needed to be dispatched.

I made it through the night. In the morning, I was informed that my surgery was scheduled for 5:00 pm. I faced a busy day. My friends came in the morning and brought sunshine with them. I was in good spirits. As my friends visited, in came the resident with the gaggle of interns behind her. Unbelievably, she said, "You've been causing a lot of excitement." I glared at her. I had that do not mess with me look on my face and steam came out of my ears. I was calm, but through gritted teeth I said, "No, the excitement was caused by you. If the intern who took my EKG knew what he was doing, I would not have been rushed to the emergency room." Her eyes got wide, and each of the interns took a step back. After some innocuous medical comment, the resident and her entourage quickly left. I turned to my friends. They were laughing. They had seen that glare before and knew it was not a good thing to be on the receiving end.

At 2:00 in the afternoon, I was subjected to a stress test. I was taken from my room and brought to cardiology. I did not like the idea that a dye would be injected into my body, but I had no choice. It was either that or postpone the surgery. After the dye was injected, a coldness took over my body. It felt like my body had been invaded. The attendant assured me that what I experienced was normal. I was unnerved. I could not help but think that my body was being overtaxed with the stress test and then surgery in a few hours. The trooper in me surfaced. Ya gotta do what ya gotta do! I made it through the stress test, and I was brought back to my room.

The time of the surgery approached. My friends prayed with me. One of them saw that I was surrounded by angels. I asked the Lord why I could not see them. I had been seeing angels since the day I was saved. The Lord assured me that I would see them as I was wheeled into the operating room. I was blessed to have my friends with me. I was not alone. One of them instructed me to say the name of Jesus as I was taken to the operating room and again when the anesthesia was to be administered. It was time. I was moved to a gurney and brought to the ante room to await surgery. While I waited, the anesthesiologist came by to introduce himself. I explained that he needed to talk to my surgeon concerning the type of anesthesia he should use. He was old school, was not happy and walked away. At that moment, my surgeon entered the area. He came over and had a smile on his face. He said, "Boy, have you been through it." I laughed. He explained what was going to happen next. I told him he should speak to the anesthesiologist. He is not happy. He smiled and went over to the other doctor. The conversation seemed a little intense. I then saw my surgeon put his hand on the anesthesiologist's shoulder. In that moment, I knew my surgeon had listened to me. He was going to stick to our plan.

I waited. I prayed quietly in the spirt. I started singing in the spirit. I was overcome with joy. I saw my angel of protection, Albert, sitting on the edge of the gurney. He smiled at me. As I was wheeled into the operating room, Jesus kept His promise. I saw a flood of angels fill the room, and I heard such a heavenly sound as they sang. It was truly heaven on earth. I sensed the Lord tell me that the ramparts of heaven were cheering me on. I had not been given any anesthesia yet. I knew I was not hallucinating. I whispered the name of Jesus. Peace flooded my spirit. I was moved to the operating table. Again, I spoke the name of Jesus. That is the last thing I remember until I woke up in recovery. When I opened my eyes, I saw my friends standing right beside me.

My doctor came into the room. He had a big smile on his face. He said, "You came through the surgery well. He said the surgery took 3 ½ hours instead of 2 hours, but everything looked good. He said that the lymph nodes and surrounding tissue looked clean. We got everything. We just had to wait for the lab report to confirm. I was so grateful, but I wanted to understand why the surgery went longer than expected. He said there was oozing that they had difficulty stopping. It was later that my friends told me that during the surgery they sensed something was up and they needed to pray. The Holy Spirit revealed I was in a spiritual battle. The oozing was caused by a spirit that had attached itself to my reproductive organs early on in my life. It did not want to let go. It was Jeanie who said, "the cancer needs to be cut out. Saying the name of Jesus twice before surgery was a critical strategy. Even demons must bow to the name of Jesus. All I could say was, "Thank you, Jesus."

I did not have any reaction to the anesthesia and the antibiotics. After 24 hours, I was released and sent home to recuperate. It was during this time that I learned how giving people can be. For four days, two of my friends took shifts and stayed with me overnight. They saw to my needs, such as cooking and laundry. One friend even accompanied me on walks to build up my stamina. They made sure I was well taken care of. I did not realize how I would need help. My friends did, and they were there for me. This was a big lesson for me in learning to receive. I did so graciously and with a thankful heart. It was also a time of witnessing answered prayer. I prayed that I would not have any pain after the surgery. I had just a little discomfort, but I had no pain. I needed six weeks to recuperate, and all went well. The best news came a few days after the surgery. The lab results showed that the cancer was completely removed. I was spared going through chemo or radiation. I cried with joy at the news. Through the whole process, deep down, I knew everything would be okay.

While my body was healing, I sensed that I was to do a run of my show beginning in June. I had a knowing deep inside that was my next step. I contacted the director of the theater, and we chatted about what it would take to do a run. It was agreed that I would perform my show on Thursday nights for seven weeks. I could hardly sit down, yet I stepped out in faith, met with the theater director, and signed the contract. My primary goal was to get critic reviews of the show and my performance. I hired a publicist to get my name out there. I was on my way.

I thought it was stressful to fill the theater for my premiere, but that stress was multiplied as I tried to fill the theater for seven performances. It did not matter. I needed to do this. I have a story to tell. The overall theme of my show, It's Only Lipstick, is that it is never too late to go after your dreams. I share my life and how the Lord showed Himself strong. I reveal how I have come into my own. I did not realize how touched people would be by the show. There were several nights when the post show Q&A turned into church. People asked questions about my faith and wanted to know more. I remember one young woman who sat in the front row. It was as if she was frozen in her seat. I went up to her after the Q&A. I sat down beside her, and we started to talk. She told me that she was afraid her dreams about being an actress would never come to pass. She was about 25. She said I helped her realize to not quit but to keep going after her dreams. She fell into my arms. I prayed with her. She just sobbed. It was then I realized it is not about church. It is not about me.

I put things in perspective. I planted seeds that not only inspired and encouraged others to go after their dreams but boldly shared how the Lord touched my life. My own show also encouraged me. I made it through so much, and I continue to pursue my own dream. I received such a confirmation that I am called to perform. My juices pump and I am exhilarated when I follow my passion. Even though I lost money on the run of my show, I looked at it as an investment in both myself and in others. For myself, that investment enabled me to get my name out there. I received wonderful reviews. One biggie was from broadwayworld.com. In a nutshell, the critic said the show was, "… touching, moving and hilarious…such heartfelt emotion…" My show was given four major blasts in broadwayworld.com. I was now ready to move to the next phase of my life.

I realized I had a message of inspiration and encouragement. Years before, my agent asked me, "Why do you want to be an actress?" I looked at her and smiled. I even filled up with emotion. I said, "I want to touch people whether it be through laughter or tears. I want to touch hearts." That is exactly what I am doing. I started to use my voice. I continued to spread the message of my show through a blog. The whole premise of my blog was to encourage and inspire others with a little laughter along the way. I would share my life experiences, the lessons learned and how they led to my following my own dream of being an actress. I was so touched when I would receive feedback from readers on how my articles spoke to them. I received one email from a college student who was up at 1:00 in the morning reading my article. She said it brought her to tears. She said it felt like I was writing just for her. I find it interesting how young people gravitate to my no-nonsense approach to life. Maybe it is because I am not mom. People appreciate my honesty. I appreciate my honesty. I have described myself as "all stuff an no fluff." I am loving, and I speak the truth. I am an honest voice in a world deluged by falsehoods. My faith is based on God's absolute truth and drives me to do what I know to do. In truth, I keep moving forward. I keep believing. I keep taking steps of faith. I keep trusting. I keep discovering.

Chapter 16
I Am Who I Am

My show propelled me into embracing who I am. I discovered I was made of strontg stuff. I beat cancer. I was bouncing back from the accident. I found my voice. I had confidence in myself as an actress and a writer. I am now a butterfly. I felt the future looked bright. I believe that I planted seeds into my destiny and am following my purpose. When I jumped off that cliff into the arms of Jesus, I just knew deep within me that my future is definitely in His hands. The Lord used Dr. Michelle Corral to let me know He had a plan for me. She prophesied that the Lord would bring non-believers into my life who would be a strong source of support. That very week, a producer strolled into my life that I met a few years before when I auditioned for and booked a role for a staged reading. I believe in staying in touch with people, and I invited him to come to my show. He came on the second night of the run. At the end of the performance, he came up to me and just hugged me. He kept hugging me and telling me how talented I am. I felt a bit awkward, but I relished the moment. Little did I know this producer, director, writer, and actor named Lonnie Hughes would become my mentor and a trusted friend.

I knew Dr. Corral prophesied about Lonnie. My show closed in August, and Lonnie and I reconnected in October 2017. We met over tea, and we just clicked. The conversation was open and easy. Now that my show was finished, he asked me if I was working on anything else. I mentioned that I had written the pilot for my sitcom, as well, as the logline/one sheet which summarizes the show and the show bible which breaks down the show and character descriptions. He found the concept of the show compelling and asked if I would send them to him. He offered to look them over and give me his feedback. I agreed. I was stunned by what happened next. He told me he loved the pilot.

It was funny and well-written, but the logline/one sheet and the show bible needed to be strengthened. In a selfless act of kindness, Lonnie offered to help me rework them to make them more compelling. To have someone offer to work with me was mind blowing. I accepted his kind offer.

I did not know how hard Lonnie would push me. He saw something in me and would not allow me to settle for mediocre. I have always pushed myself to excellence, but it was different having someone else do it. Over a period of three months, there were times I cried. There were times I shut down. There were times I would say, "I need to digest that" after being given constructive criticism that I was not ready to receive. There were times we would have strong disagreements that, in the past, would have crushed me. Lonnie understands the creative process. I was now in the deep end of the pool. I was not sure how to swim. I was used to being the mentor. I was now on the receiving end. Lonnie has such patience and he allowed me to make discoveries and learn about being an artist. I had to die to my preconceived notions and grow as a writer and as a person. I also discovered that I grew as an actress. Ripping the characters down to the bare bones enabled me to get a greater depth of understanding in character development. I thank God for this collaboration. We both came out unscathed and have a greater appreciation for the work and each other. We are excited about the finished work and look forward to where we can take it.

I had an epiphany. I now understand mutual respect. Lonnie respects me, and I respect him. I also respect myself. I would carry this epiphany over into three other friendships. I needed friendship, and often entered into them without checking in with the Lord first. Initially, I did not know each person was co-dependent. As I had grown, my eyes were opened, and I put a stop to being used and abused. One friend was injured. I would run errands for her and take her to physical therapy. She was hurting financially, and I would buy groceries for her. The last straw was when she told me she did not have money for gas, so I would take her where she needed to go. I later discovered she was driving miles to meet with another friend. I could feel a stirring deep inside that something was off. I sent her an email and laid out what was on my mind. She never got back to me. I knew the friendship was over. I let her go.

I parted ways with another friend who constantly blamed me for things. Before the Lord healed me; I accepted the blame. One day we had brunch. She asked my opinion about what do financially. She set up a website to generate residual income. She was almost finished with it. She told me she signed up to take a course for directing. It cost $500. I suggested that she finish setting up her website and, once it started to generate income, she should then take the course for directing. It was as if a thunderstorm descended on our brunch. She got quiet. She ended the brunch. I texted her. She went on a rant about how I stole her dream. I know about going after dreams. There is no way I would steal anyone's dream from them. The texts got worse. I called her instead. I had grown so confident in myself that I wanted to deal with this either over the phone or face to face. No response. I let her go.

The third friendship was a bit more complicated. We were friends before and then separated. I did not understand why we did. Apparently, I did something heinous. Our paths crossed again at a church service. She came over an apologized and asked me to forgive her. I did so without question. The problem came when I let her back into my life without praying about it first. Things seemed to be going fine. She was with me during the surgery and helped me out afterwards. I will always be grateful. Again, things got bizarre. For no reason, she stopped talking to me. I tried to contact her. Nothing. I saw her at church. She walked away. I let her go. As I ended these friendships, I learned I had gained respect for myself, and I would not tolerate anyone tearing me down. If I make a mistake, I am quick to apologize. I will no longer take responsibility for another person's dreck. I sought prayer. I learned that when we let people into our lives there are soul ties. We get connected. I needed to be free of them and my old self.

I moved forward. I kept shedding those things that held me back. Just as the walls of Jericho came down with shout, so did mine. It may have taken years, but it was time to see myself for who I am. My wall reflects me. It was time to see that my wall is red. It is bold. It is colorful. It is powerful. It radiates my voice. It radiates me. It radiates the blood of Jesus that has set me free. It has been a journey, but I tore down the walls that blocked me from coming into my own. I have come to not only like myself but love myself.

I needed to be in this place. The Lord has given me a vision of my destiny. I have written the vision down. I have received many prophetic words that confirmed what I knew the Lord told me. Many of those words said things would happen soon. I have learned that my soon and God's soon are two very different things. I was ready to hit the ground running. My sitcom was in a great place and ready to be pitched. With Lonnie's help, there were some open doors that shut rather quickly. I only booked one role as a judge for a TV show. Auditions were few and far between. I did everything I know to do. I often said, "Lord, now is a good time for you to show up and show off." I was ready to run. Instead, I sensed, "be still and know that I am God." (Psalm 46:10, NKJV) I was not happy.

I may have emerged as a butterfly, but I needed direction on where to fly. I sensed I was to move to another church. It was quick. I spoke with Dr. Corral, and I received her blessing. I had a friend who attended the church, so I was not going in cold. When I arrived, I was surprised to find someone there that I befriended in Torah class. We connected very quickly, and she asked me to assist her in a women's group that the Lord had impressed upon her to start. I prayed about it, and I got the green light. Just as Joshua and Caleb held up the arms of Moses, I soon learned I was to be her Joshua. My life experiences in business, creatively and in the church enabled me to counsel her on different issues. I felt blessed to be there for her and the women.

Suddenly, I sensed I was to bring my show back for SoloFest 2020. I hungered to be on stage, but I was conflicted. I was concerned about the money I needed to produce the show. I battled. I told the Lord I did not want to do it. He won. I contacted the show coordinator and filed the paperwork. I was approved within a couple of hours. I sensed I was to stand on Psalm 23, so I requested January 23rd as my performance date. Now that the date was set, I was grateful I did not have to start from scratch. The show was written. I amazed myself that I had most of the show still memorized. I had grown as a writer, and I changed the show a bit to give it more impact. I contacted my former Technical Director, and he helped me develop my promotional materials. I learned how to market my show through social media, and I was able to promote the show through the church website.

Things fell into place, except I started to stress about the lack of ticket sales. The show date was approaching, and I was nowhere near the ticket sales I needed to break even. I knew the Lord wanted me to bring the show back. I finally said, "Lord, I trust you. Have a good time." Once I decided to trust Him, I felt a new freedom to focus on the show and enjoy myself. This time was different. I was free. I had come through so much. This time I did not have the fear of cancer hanging over me. My show is very physical. I rehearsed and rehearsed and rehearsed. The intense physical activity strained my right foot. Two weeks before the show I could not walk. I was in so much pain. I prayed. I sought medical help. The doctor said I needed to stay off my foot. How was I supposed to do that? I did the unthinkable. I took Aleve to ease the pain.

Show day arrived. I once again went through four hours of setting up the technical part of the show and two run throughs. When we finished, I was limping. I did my ritual and prayed over and anointed each seat and doorway in the theater. I waited backstage. I was excited, but trepidatious at the same time. Would I be able to perform full throttle with foot pain? Even taking the Aleve, I still had pain. I started to hear the audience move into the theater. It sounded like there were a lot of people. The lights came down, and I took my place on stage. I once heard a preacher say, "Walking with the Lord is like a chess match. We move, then He moves." By listening to the Holy Spirit within me, I was not alone. I felt His presence on stage with me throughout the show. I lived and relished each and every moment. I performed for 95 minutes straight without any physical problem. I had a blast and so did the audience. The moment I hit the stage all the pain in my foot disappeared. I made a move. In faith, I showed up and the Lord showed off.

I soon learned why the Lord wanted me to do my show again. When I left New York, I never spoke to my pastors again. My heart was heavy that I left on a negative note. I prayed for the Lord to restore the relationship. Although the pastor passed away, I reconnected with my pastor's wife, sixteen years later. I promoted my show through social media. She saw the promo on Facebook that I was going to livestream my performance from the theater. To my delight, she watched it. She called me the next day to tell me how much she enjoyed it. We spoke for almost two hours. It was like we had never lost touch. In the conversation, she asked me to forgive them if they did anything that might have hurt me. I forgave them years ago. That heart of forgiveness enabled me to talk with her as if nothing happened. I am grateful that she is back in my life. I believe the Lord used this as a sign that He will keep His Word, "I will restore to you the years the swarming locust has eaten…" (Joel 2:25, NKJV)

I received a surprise. Jessica Lynn Johnson invited me to give an encore performance in the Solo Show Series of Stars at a different theater in Hollywood. I was delighted to be considered for such an event. I prayed about it. I accepted. As I started to develop the marketing materials to promote my show, I made a wonderful discovery. I figured out how to use a computer program to take my existing materials and make the necessary changes. This was huge. This meant I was bouncing back from the cognitive inability to process information. It took me awhile to recreate the materials, but I did it. If I could have done a cartwheel, I would have. I sensed to perform my encore on February 8, 2020. I came alive when I performed. It was exhilarating to be on stage again, even though I did not quite cover my expenses. I knew I was doing what I was called to do. I wanted to keep doing it. Then, Covid-19 brought down the curtain across the world.

I was frightened. I hunkered down like everyone else. I prayed. I cried as I watched the world shut its doors and withdraw from the outside world. I needed people. I discovered Zoom. I was able to socialize and get my mind off the tragedy that surrounded me. People today do not believe me when I tell them how introverted I was. They see a confident woman who has allowed herself to be transformed by the goodness of God. Through the lockdown, I took classes on how to move forward in my life and career. I attended workshops with industry professionals. I built my website. I focused on my spiritual life. I joined prayer meetings. I was able to put others before myself. I prayed for and encouraged others. It was also a time of great reflection. I look at my life now and am grateful I am not the person I used to be. I allowed myself to be transformed. I did not like who I was. I know what God promised in His Word, and that is what I wanted. I allowed myself to go through the pain of change. I allowed myself to believe that God has better for me. I allowed myself to believe that there is a purpose for my life. My desire goes beyond being an actress. It is to touch a life whether it be through tears or laughter. If I can inspire and encourage one person, I am beyond happy. If I can help someone believe in themselves that they and their dreams matter, I am beyond happy. It has not been an easy journey. But I have found that through my experiences, I can be empathetic to what people are going through. I can be what they need, whether it be love, strength, or even constructive criticism.

As the lockdown continued, the isolation started to impact me. I battled to encourage myself. I listened to uplifting messages online. I spoke to family and friends. During a prayer meeting, I received a prophetic word to put my show online. I received that word not once, but five different times. I sensed I was to do that, but the Lord used others to get my attention. I was willing, but I had no clue as to how to put my show online. One of the leaders in my church home group works with visual effects. He volunteered to help me. It took several weeks, but I finally put my show up. I believed that I heard God and trusted that I was following His guidance. I promoted my show. I kept promoting it. I did not get the viewership I wanted or needed. I was frustrated. Why does it seem that nothing works out for me? Instead of looking at God, I looked at the circumstances. I did that woe is me thing. The Covid-19 lockdown became my second life-changing event. This time it was a spiritual. I had a wrestling match with God. It was a battle in my mind. I know what God promised me, but I started to believe that His promises would not come to pass. I felt I was fooling myself. I got real with God. I have been following my dream for 18 years. I grew tired of words. I needed proof. I broke down and sobbed and sobbed and sobbed. I invested so much of myself into my dream. I had no idea what I would do other than acting. I was spent. I cried out to God in my journal. "Help me get my peace back. Help me to continue to trust you. Help me with strategies and wisdom. I need you to invade my mind, my heart, and my spirit to trust You."

I was in a broken place. The Lord touched me and began to heal the broken places. I was on the potter's wheel. I had a vision of myself as a pottery vessel and there were cracks in it. I then saw liquid gold pour into the vessel from heaven and fill the cracks. The following day, I attended a women's group through Zoom. The leader of the group started talked about Kintsugi. I never heard of it. It is a

Japanese technique of filling cracks in pottery with liquid gold, silver, or gemstones. The pottery becomes even more valuable. I was so moved that the Lord showed me that through my brokenness I have become more valuable. My tears turned into laughter. I, once again, used poetry to express my deep emotion.

CRACKED UP

Suddenly before my eyes
A vision given by You my Lord and You don't lie
I saw myself as a broken vessel
After years being ground by mortar and pestle
I saw You pouring out liquid gold from heaven
Liquid gold filling every crack and broken place
A glistening of liquid love filling every space
In a single moment, the pain of the past erased by unconditional love
Replaced with a joy that cracked me up
Tears streaming down my face
As I beheld how You see me
Refined as pure gold for all to see
I am Your masterpiece
Fearfully and wonderfully made
Rising up out of the ashes
Wearing a garland of sweet praise
Overcome with the Light of Love within me
Overwhelmed with joy
Bathed in a peace
Laughing so hard it hurts
Laughter from deep within

Lighting up every fiber of my being

Allowing myself to just bask in Your presence

Just You and Me

My heart filled with gratitude

As I know I am changed

I am new

All because of You

It is a new day

A new season

A season of coming into the fullness of

Who Am I

I have come through the fire

Stepping confidently into the dreams You inspired

For years sitting at Your feet

Now seeing I'm seated at your banqueting table

Able to freely sup

Fully satisfied and all cracked up

Written by Claudia DiMartino 6/14/20

I soon realized that deep healing would continue. Two months later, I attended Sunday service online. The pastor prayed at the end. I broke down. I did not know I was holding onto anger toward the doctors who prescribed steroids to me over 28 years ago. A few days later, I journaled, "I've been sobbing for days. It is coming from deep within. I am sensing I am mourning all those things I have lost. You are cleansing me of the pain of the past. What amazes me, that during this time of upheaval, You use me to bless others. I have even written a few poems. I desperately need you, Abba. I feel You bringing me to a place of completely trusting You. I am in pain, Abba. Help me get through this."

A few days later, I listened to a minister online. I was sort of listening because I was familiar with what he was teaching. Then, he got my attention. He talked about the seed of the woman. Women do not have seeds. They have eggs. In Genesis, scripture says, I will put enmity between your seed and the seed of the woman. He started talking about God's seed is Jesus. It was by the Holy Spirit that Mary was impregnated. There was nothing of man's carnality in the conception. Then, he talked about how Isaac and John the Baptist were God's seeds because both Sarah and Elizabeth were barren. It was miraculous that they conceived. The children were filled with the Holy Spirit. He talked about when he wants to be one with God, he abstains from sexual relations with his wife. No carnal activity. Then it hit me. I journaled, "I have never given into carnal desires. I have never known a man. I started crying because I started sensing that I am filled with the Holy Spirit. You are the only one I have loved. Then I started to sense to lay down all the desires of my heart. You need me to be completely focused on You. I started to sob. I then sensed that these last few weeks of mourning and sobbing have been me dying to the flesh. I have reached a new level of trusting You, Abba. I need Your help with this. I choose to lay it all down at the foot of the cross. I choose you, Abba. I choose You, Jesus. I choose You, Holy Spirit. You are my everything." In that moment, I had a oneness with the Lord. He is truly my first love. His love poured through me and enabled me to love myself. As I laid everything down before the Lord, I confess there was a twinge of humanness. I still have desires to be an actress and to marry. He reminded me that He put those desires in me. He reminded me of the scripture, "Delight yourself in the Lord and He shall give you the desires of your heart." (Psalm 37:4, NKJV) As I process all of this, I realize that this deep cleansing happened the month before Rosh Hashanah. It was the month of Elul. The month of getting right with God before the Jewish New Year.

On Rosh Hashanah, I was joyful. I had come through a difficult time of cleansing before the Lord. I was expectant for the new year. Circumstances had not changed. We were still in lockdown due to Covid-19. I was not sure what was next. I just knew that I was in good hands. What I found interesting is that I started smelling toast. At times, the smell was so strong. I looked up the spiritual significance of smelling toast through Bob Jones University. The smell of toast means being slammed by God. That is exactly what was happening to me. I felt the weightiness of God's presence. There were times I could hardly stand. I laughed in the Spirit. I wept as I worshipped. I was in heaven. Then, on December 21st, the day the Bethlehem star was the most visible in the sky, the Lord gave me a prophetic word for me through me. I sensed to record it. In a nutshell, the Lord has increased the anointing and mantle on my life. He said that when I declare God's Word, I should expect to see the manifestation in the authority of Jesus' name. I would also be used to release joy and I was being taken out of hiding. I was undone by this prophetic word. I sent it to Jeanie Richardson and asked her to be a witness to it. She called me immediately and said it was from the Lord.

In the months following, I have been asked to teach in different zoom meetings. I have also been moved to a new church. I thought, "Here we go again." To my surprise, I know the pastor and his mother from the church that tried to quench the anointing in my life. The Lord used me in the past to speak words of life to them. They know me. We met and chatted about the church and how I could serve. They gave me the green light to move as the Holy Spirit leads me. At first, I was a little nervous to step out, but they have welcomed me and the spiritual gifts I carry with open arms. I have only been there for two months, but I feel like I have been there for years. I do not know if I am on an assignment. I just know I feel at home.

I am loving the surprises that have been unfolding in 2021. One of the biggest surprises is this book. Dr. Michelle Corral and others prophesied that I had books in me. I have had ideas floating around inside me. I prayed about it and sensed the Lord say, "Go back to the first book idea I gave you, My Wall Is Red." I have written poetry. I have written a show. I have written a sitcom. But I have never written a book. I was clueless to the level of soul searching and inner healing to which I was about to embark. I wrote my first draft and thought, that was not so bad. I was blissfully ignorant. I gave it to three people to read, one of them being Lonnie Hughes. He was gracious and said my book was about 80% there. When it comes to Lonnie, I found the thought of focusing on the other 20% scary. I was right.

Lonnie, once again, generously offered to mentor me through this process. His primary comment to me was, "I feel you are holding back. I want to feel what you are feeling." I thought I did that. I was not even close. He said, "Anyone can be a writer. Not everyone is willing to be an artist." I think I now have a window of understanding as to why Van Gogh cut off his ear. He stayed with me word for word, line by line, paragraph by paragraph and chapter by chapter. He has stayed with me through the emotional rollercoaster and encouraged me to keep going. This has been a journey of discovery. Things I buried so deep came to the surface. Things I have never told anyone became cornerstones for me to be raw and real. There were days the pain of remembrance was so deep, I needed to walk away. I needed to go for a walk or a drive. I needed to go to a movie, but they were not open yet due to the pandemic. I needed to be alone with God. I needed to let Him pick me up off the floor and strengthen me to continue. I needed to let my life unfold before me to witness the miracle that I am today.

The Lord has transformed this once frightened, insecure, introverted little girl and blossomed me into a strong, confident woman. It took the healing hand of God and losing my ovaries to recognize that I am a woman. This is a new concept for me. This hit home on my birthday. Lonnie asked me what I wanted for my birthday. I could sense the Holy Spirit say, "Ask him." I said nothing. Again, Lonnie asked me, "What do you want for your birthday"? The Holy Spirit prompted me again, "Ask him." I took a deep breath and asked Lonnie if he would clean out my garden. My physical challenges make it difficult for me to do it myself. Also, what I know about gardening, I can fit on the head of a pin. Lonnie just looked at me with this big smile on his face. He said he would love to do that for me. I did not know that he loves to be out in the garden. It gives him such peace. It was, as if in that moment, I was healed of the memories of my father refusing to do things my mother asked him to do. They seemed to melt away.

I was excited that my garden would be cleaned out and free of brush and debris. I got things ready for the big event. Or so I thought. I bought extra-large trash bags. I had clippers. I had a broom and borrowed a rake. Lonnie showed up on time and ready to go. The supplies I provided were unfit at best. I tried to borrow a trash can. I could not. The clippers I had were inadequate. The thorns cut into

Lonnie's hands. I ran out to a gardening store. They did not have any trash cans in stock. I purchased clippers and gardening gloves. The gardening gloves worked, but the clippers did not. I needed to purchase shears. I did not know there was a difference. I ran back to the store to make the exchange. I felt badly that my lack of knowledge slowed things down. Lonnie was a trooper. It took hours, and the sun was setting. He stayed with it and finished the job.

As Lonnie removed trash bag after trash bag, I started to prepare dinner. This I knew how to do. The table was set, and I had all the ingredients on hand from appetizers to dessert. I know he has a thing for anchovies. I blessed him and prepared my mother's recipe for pasta with anchovy sauce. As I milled around in the kitchen, Lonnie came in from outside. He was so sweaty and dirty from hours of hard labor. He had asked me prior to coming over if he would be able to shower when he finished up. I agreed. I was now faced with an uncomfortable situation. A man I am not married to is going to be in my spare bathroom taking a shower. Was I going to be a woman or a child? I chose to be woman. I knew I was safe with Lonnie, and I can trust him. I walked him to the bathroom and showed him the different towels he might need. I went back to the kitchen and continued preparing dinner.

If I learned anything from my mother, it is how to be the hostess with the mostest. When Lonnie emerged all squeaky clean from the bathroom, I had appetizers waiting for him in the living room. As he came into the room, I was standing. I wondered if I should tell him about the showering in my apartment thing. I did. He just looked at me and said, "I know." He moved into the living room, sat down, and became wide eyed looking at the bruschetta I made from scratch. I said enjoy as I still milled about playing hostess. Suddenly, Lonnie broke the silence and complimented me. He said, "You are beautiful." I stopped. I looked at him. I started to cry. I said, "You are the only man other than my father who has said I am beautiful." To say that shocked him is an understatement. It shocked me even more. I did not know quite how to receive this compliment. It made me uncomfortable. I am still a work in progress. I am in a new phase of my life. It is unfolding before me as I discover the layers of me that were buried and are rising to the surface. On my birthday, I unwrapped the gift that I have more of my mother in me than I thought. I thoroughly enjoyed preparing dinner for Lonnie. I understood the joy my mother had every day as she expressed her love by cooking for her family. We became one. On my birthday, I unwrapped the gift of true friendship. I let the little girl go and decided to trust a man. As I unwrapped this gift, I dismantled the fear of men from my wall. On my birthday, I removed the sign "Don't touch." Dare I wonder if this was a rehearsal as the Lord is preparing me for the husband He has in the wings. Lonnie said, "Today felt like we were married. We are so in sync." The friendship I discovered with Lonnie amplifies the marriage, friendship, and relationship I have with the Lord. I have been rehearsing for years.

My life is still unfolding. I am willing to be an active participant. As I enter this new phase, I realize I have emerged from the cleft of the rock stronger. I am an eagle, and I am ready to fly higher and see further. The Lord knew what He was doing when He created me. "I am fearfully and wonderfully made." (Psalm 139:14, NKJV). He made me to be uniquely me and reflect who He is in me. I have discovered many do not understand the path I am following. That is okay. It may seem odd for me to write a memoir when I have not yet come to the fullness of my destiny. When I think of the cultural worldview of my life, people might say I have not been successful. But I am. I have come to the place of succeeding at who I am. I may not be where I am going, but I am not where I was, and I accept me where I am. It is a day to day walk of faith. I rejoice that I had the courage to pursue my lifelong dream and the conviction to not compromise what I believe. I have had the strength of character to let people go from my life that were bringing me down. I have learned to respect myself, and I expect others to do the same. I am now willing to receive the love and encouragement from family and friends. It has taken a lifetime for me trust people. First, I had to choose to trust God. I had to lose everything to know that I am not alone. I trust His Word. "…because God has said, "Never will I leave you; never will I forsake you." (Hebrews 13:5, NIV) He has brought people into my life that accept me for me, and I can trust that they have my back.

In choosing to trust the Lord, I now can rejoice that my relationship with Him has grown into the place that each day I am dancing with Jesus, and I am letting him lead. The Lord has given me a vision of where I am going. I believe He will get me there. I do not know how. I do not know when. I just know that I should look to Him and not my circumstances. There are days that "building yourself up in your most holy faith." (Jude 1:20, NIV) rings loudly for me. That is okay. If I get a little shaky or mess up, it does not mean the Lord is angry with me and will punish me. I ask for forgiveness with the understanding that His love is unconditional. Years ago, I walked away from religion. I have found relationship. It is sweet. It is all consuming. It is forever.

I am living out my destiny. I am living out my dreams. I believe what the Lord has told me. I believe that I am a vessel used to bring joy and laughter into the world. Each day is an adventure in the Lord. Each day the sun comes up. Each day brings new hope. Each day I can walk in the joy that I am who I am. Each day I accept that I am not like anyone else. This confidence has blossomed out of my relationship with the Lord. This confidence has resulted in stronger relationships with others. I have torn down the walls that were built on lies. I know the truth. Out of the ashes has come beauty. "I am truly His rose, the very theme of His song. I am overshadowed by His love, like a lily growing in the valley! (Song of Songs 2:1, TPT) I think the greatest gift I received is that I now see myself through my Father's eyes. I wrote this poem over eleven years ago. It has taken that long to take root in my spirit.

The Lily

The lily is a flower that I did not embrace I love color.

In my life, the lily seemed out of place

Yet, in recent days, You have shown me

That in your eyes, I am the lily

The lily? I don't understand

Come close. Take my hand

And behold the lily. Beautiful and strong.

A fighter. An overcomer.

Shaped by the difficulties of life

Emerging with a new song

The song of the bride

With the purity of white

Without blemish or wrinkle

So pleasing in sight

Handpicked for the bridal bouquet

Behold the lily and say

I see myself with Your eyes

Perfected by love and without a flaw

Written by: Claudia DiMartino – 4/4/2013

I believe that I am in a new season. "Can you not discern this new day of destiny breaking forth around you? The early signs of my purposes and plans are bursting forth. The budding vines of new life are now blooming everywhere. The fragrance of their flowers whispers, 'there is change in the air.' Arise my love, my beautiful companion, and run with me to the higher place. For now is the time to arise and come away with me." (Song of Songs 2:13, TPT) I have been transformed and so has my wall. My wall now reflects love. My wall now reflects strength. My wall now reflects joy. My wall now reflects the truth of who and Whose I am. My wall reflects me. I can now look up with a grateful heart and declare victory. I declare that My Wall is Red.

About the Author

Claudia DiMartino grew up in an Italian American family and called New York City home. Growing up in a family of immigrants, the American Dream was pursued with fervor. Claudia was no exception. She received her M.B.A in Management from Pace University's Lubin School of Business and her B.BA in Marketing from Bernard Baruch College. She worked as a Marketing Executive in the beauty industry for 22 years. In 2011, a life-changing event triggered her to pursue her childhood dream of acting. She has appeared in TV and film, as well as, written, produced, and performed in her critically acclaimed one-woman show, It's Only Lipstick. As she pursued first the American Dream and then her childhood dream, she has been on a spiritual journey which began in earnest when she had a supernatural encounter in Israel. She has discovered relationship instead of religion. She has taken steps of faith to walk out her destiny both in her career and spiritually. Discovering her voice has enabled her to minister prophetically to encourage and edify others.

Family picture

My grandmother – Rose

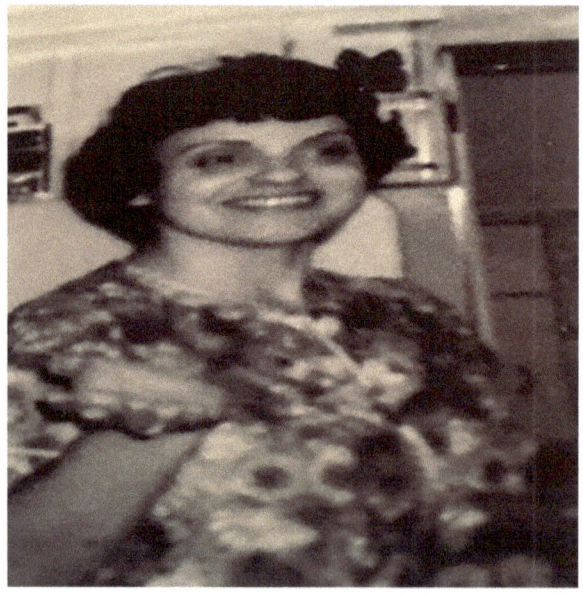

My mother – Gloria

My father – Ralph

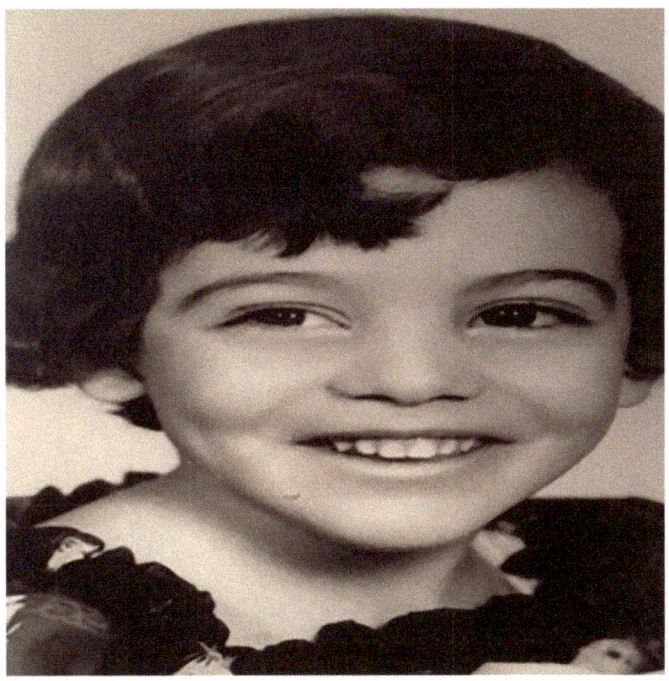

My sister - Deborah

Me - Claudia

My Aunt Dolores

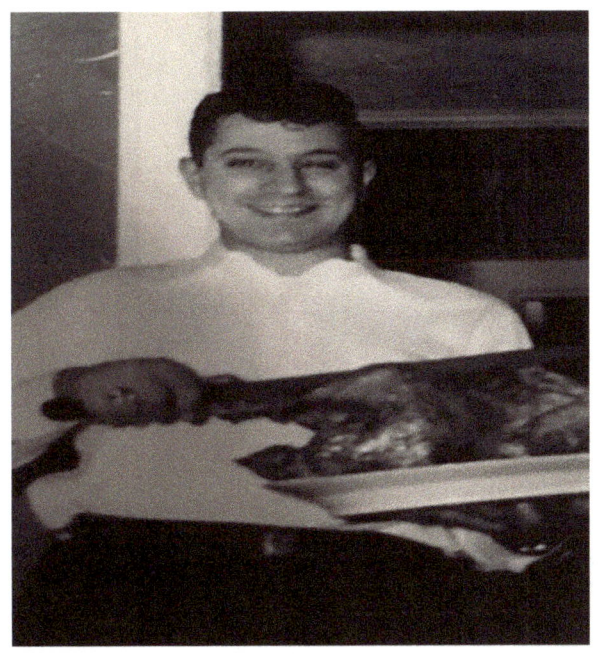

My Uncle Teddy

My cousin Wayne

My cousin - Mark

My step grandfather – Alex

www.ingramcontent.com/pod-product-compliance
Lightning Source LLC
Chambersburg PA
CBHW051149120626
46547CB00012B/1015